E A R T H

W O R K S

EARTH WORKS

HOUSES BY BYOUNG CHO

T&H

CONTENTS

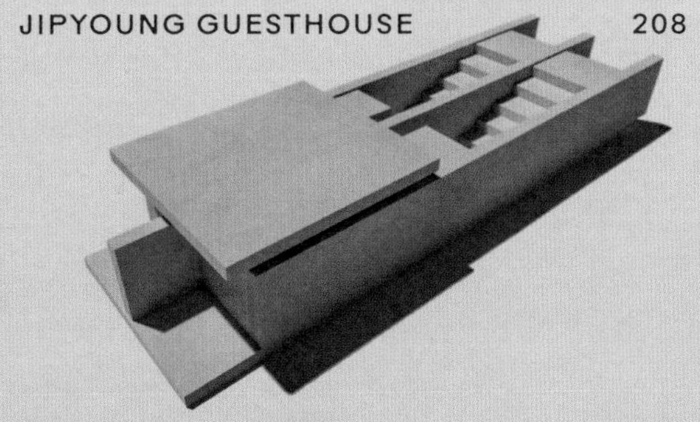

INTRODUCTION

Earth Works is the story of my belief in the earth, and how that belief has shaped my practice. I would like to tell this story by looking at some projects I have built.

My vision begins with the idea of Earth as a silent and enduring presence. While it has never been born itself, it gives birth to others. Created without life, it is eternal, while quietly witnessing the deaths of those to whom it has given birth. Any explanation or understanding of the earth must be formed by connecting it to the infinite number of other stories about the earth.

The story of the earth is the story of the sky that we gaze up at. It is the story of the breeze that dances over the earth and the cloud that drifts by, leaving the earth in its wake. It is the story of rain, the whispers of conversations, the birth of creatures, great and small. It is the story of all this and the architecture that it sustains. These stories cannot be told in isolation from the earth, as they speak of us and our history, of ourselves – those whose lives are intertwined and enmeshed.

This story is as wide as the universe. However many methods of exploration are employed, I will always fall short. It is a story that differs depending on the time and the place, on the people and their culture, and so here I look at specific examples of structures I have built, to reflect on my commitment to the earth and the practice of land architecture.

I must begin with a story from when I was young – the first time I encountered a space that made a lasting impression on me. It was a square of red earth that contrasted with the unusually clear, bright-blue Korean sky. Dug with a square, sharp-edged, angled spade, it had four straight edges and a red centre nibbled by the warm sun.

It was the home to which my friend's mother could return, the place her coffin would be laid to rest. That intense and primitive space, exhilaratingly beautiful in its clean straight lines, left a striking imprint on my soul and on my flesh and bones, one enduring memory among many that made their mark during my teenage years. I wonder whether the impulse to excavate and go into the earth is innately human, an instinct we have always carried deep within us.

The architecture I believe in does not seek to conquer the earth or triumph over it. Instead, at times it turns with the earth, and at other times it winds around the earth, submitting to the alluvial flow. For architecture that is truly compliant with the earth, an understanding of the characteristics and flow of energy is needed – of the flow and patterns of its slopes, of the flow and directions of the air, of the flow of light and, on occasion, the cycles of plant life. It is only when we truly love and submit ourselves to the earth that we may attempt to create earth works.

'Earth works' is a term and a concept I began formulating around 2015, when I was invited to present a selection of my residential projects spanning the previous two decades. With this expression, I sought to describe an architecture that emerges from the earth itself – one that reflects its conditions, embodies its phenomena, and resonates with its ever-changing flows. It is not merely about building on the land, but building with it, in dialogue with its essence.

In the most beautiful places, architecture materializes in harmony with its environment. Discreetly leaning against the side of a hill, or placed as though climbing the swell of a wave, it sits visible, yet is still at one with its surroundings. Air and light and space and time will enter it as it sits there, making it one with its surroundings. In this way, architecture that is of the earth begins with the earth, and returns to the earth, and it becomes a part of the earth.

Architecture must be simple. It must be as simple as the earth, so that it can become part of the earth. This simplicity must be defined in relation to the structure of the space, the materials used, and sometimes even in relation to the structure itself or the construction methods employed.

In this way, my earth works were born of my absolute trust and faith in our terra firma. They arise from the conviction that we must pursue a wiser form of architecture, one more attuned to the environment and shaped by the forms nature provides. This is the story of building small homes that are in tune with the flow of air, water and light, homes in which to live larger lives. And so, it follows that these earth works are not lofty ideals but rather specific, economical, simple and down-to-earth forms of architecture. At times, they represent an architecture of less, and this 'less' is not a deliberately contrived void but a natural and organic absence, one that allows for co-existence and might naturally fill over time.
As in nature, each organism has an inherent dependency on its surroundings, so the philosophical foundation of holistic sustainable architecture must be based on an understanding of the need for the built environment to co-exist in a similar way, with an inherent dependency on its surroundings.
At the same time, it must respond to tradition and

contemporary reality, becoming a breed of architecture that will exist in the inescapable embrace of these three things, just as its occupants do. This architecture represents the ultimate ideal in sustainability and is the fullest expression of what holistic sustainable architecture can be.

EXPLANATION OF THE NAMES OF THE BUILDINGS

At the start of our practice, we set out to create work that was influenced by both traditional Korean and more Western and modern architectural styles. I have a particular fondness for the shapes of traditional Korean homes, which are typically linear structures built out into the shapes of the letters I, L and U. Whereas Western architecture tends to be relatively centralized and multi-storeyed, traditional Korean architecture is spread out over a single, rather linear layer. The shapes of the homes are very diverse, but the general concepts are always the same – a combination of an open system of rooms (sometimes connected with corridors and at times simply leading directly from one room to the next), punctuated by empty space, i.e. small courtyards.

This layout responds to the climate of Korea, which experiences all four seasons intensely, with especially hot and humid summers, necessitating good ventilation. The style is also undeniably influenced by traditional Korean notions of the natural and spiritual worlds.

Belief in the influences of the divine, as well as legends and superstitions about the wilderness, shaped much of traditional Korean daily life. This can be seen in the poetry of the ancient dynasties, going back thousands of years. And it persists in our culture today – people get a huge amount of pleasure from being in nature.

I started to investigate these fundamental Korean housing shapes, traditionally named after the Hangul letters ㄴ, ㄷ and ㅁ, as well as being known by the English letters and shapes I, L, U and square. The houses of the poor were, of course, cheaper and simpler, while the houses of the rich were more complex, with greater variety. This influence in our work is particularly evident in the Concrete Box House, a single-storey structure with an empty central open-air space; the L-Shaped House, which has a long exterior walkway connecting individual units; and the Lee Oisoo House (also known as the Fish-Shaped House), with its linear, curved and string-like forms.

Detail of a concrete wall at Jipyoung Guesthouse, Geoje, South Gyeongsang Province.

2 0 0 4

T H R E E

B O X

H O U S E

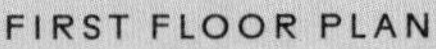

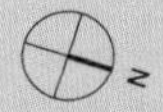

1. Master bedroom
2. Bathroom
3. Bedroom
4. Kitchen
5. Living room
6. Tea room
7. Deck
8. Studio

0 5m

SECTION

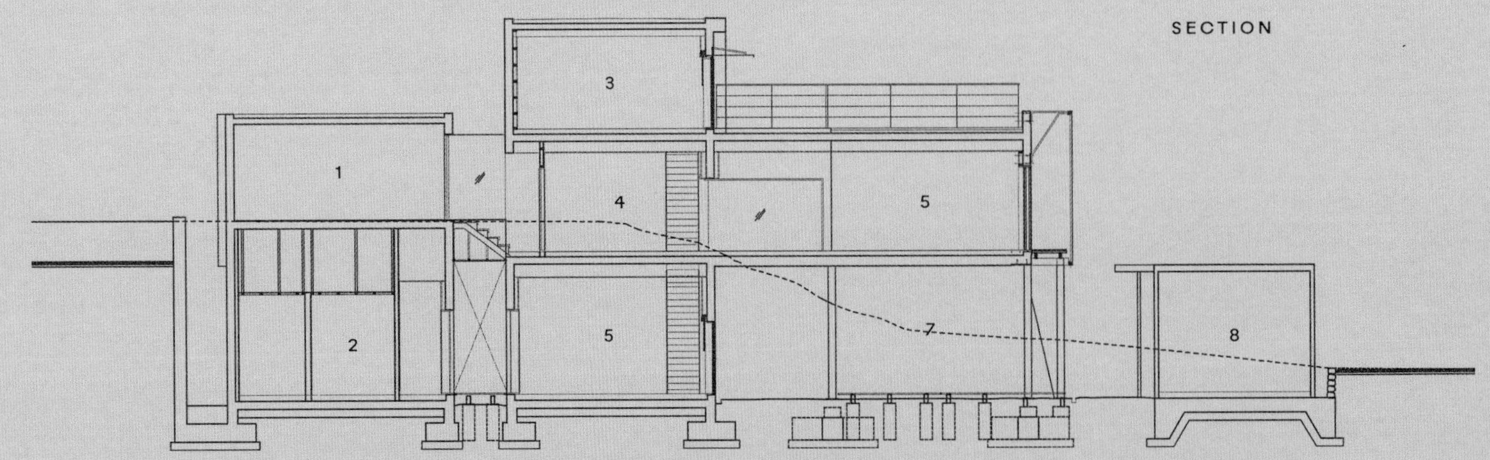

Three-Box House embodies three central paradoxes, embracing both the public and the private, the urban and the natural, the open and the enclosed. Between these extremes, the structure as a whole achieves a completeness, serving as a fluid space that inspires human interaction with nature.

The design responds to the characteristics of the site, with three concrete boxes that are strategically positioned to adapt to the varied topography while providing separation from the busy setting. Each box serves a distinct function: the first box, built into the sloping terrain, contains private rooms such as bedrooms and bathrooms, which open onto an inner courtyard; the middle box houses the main living and dining areas, with direct access to an outdoor deck and views of the surroundings; and the third box, elevated on slender metal pillars, is a flexible space for work, leisure or guests. All three volumes are aligned both horizontally and vertically, stepping up with the landscape to bridge the height difference between the lower deck and the elevated nearby roads.

Floating wooden screens connect the three concrete structures, strategically placed on the north, west and south sides to cover windows while permitting controlled visibility. In contrast, the eastern side uses a wire screen to allow ample light as well as views from the living area. The screens organize the architectural composition, gently mediating the user's experience of nature by controlling light flow and blending the structure with its surroundings.

Initially, by using a wooden screen that was easy to obtain and produce, I made it possible to experience both a private realm, sheltered from the dense urban context, and the lush natural environment. In recent years, I have spent a lot of time contemplating how to create a more environmentally friendly façade, and I have used and actively experimented with more diverse kinds of screens in the search for longer-term sustainable solutions.

LOCATION
Beopheung-ri, Tanhyeon-myeon, Paju-si, Gyeonggi-do, South Korea

GROSS FLOOR AREA
231.1 m^2 (2,488 sq. ft)

STRUCTURE
Reinforced concrete, exposed concrete finish

BELOW
The entrance is at the top of the house, which was designed to respond to the varied topography of the site.

OVERLEAF
The driveway (above) and entrance (below).

P. 23
A connecting door provides direct access from the garage.

ABOVE AND OPPOSITE
First-floor landing, with views of the courtyard and deck, and the ground-floor stairwell.

PP. 26–29
One of the boxes is elevated on metal pillars, creating space for an outdoor seating area below, as well as a separate studio.

C O N C
R E T E

B O X

H O U S E

2 0 0 4

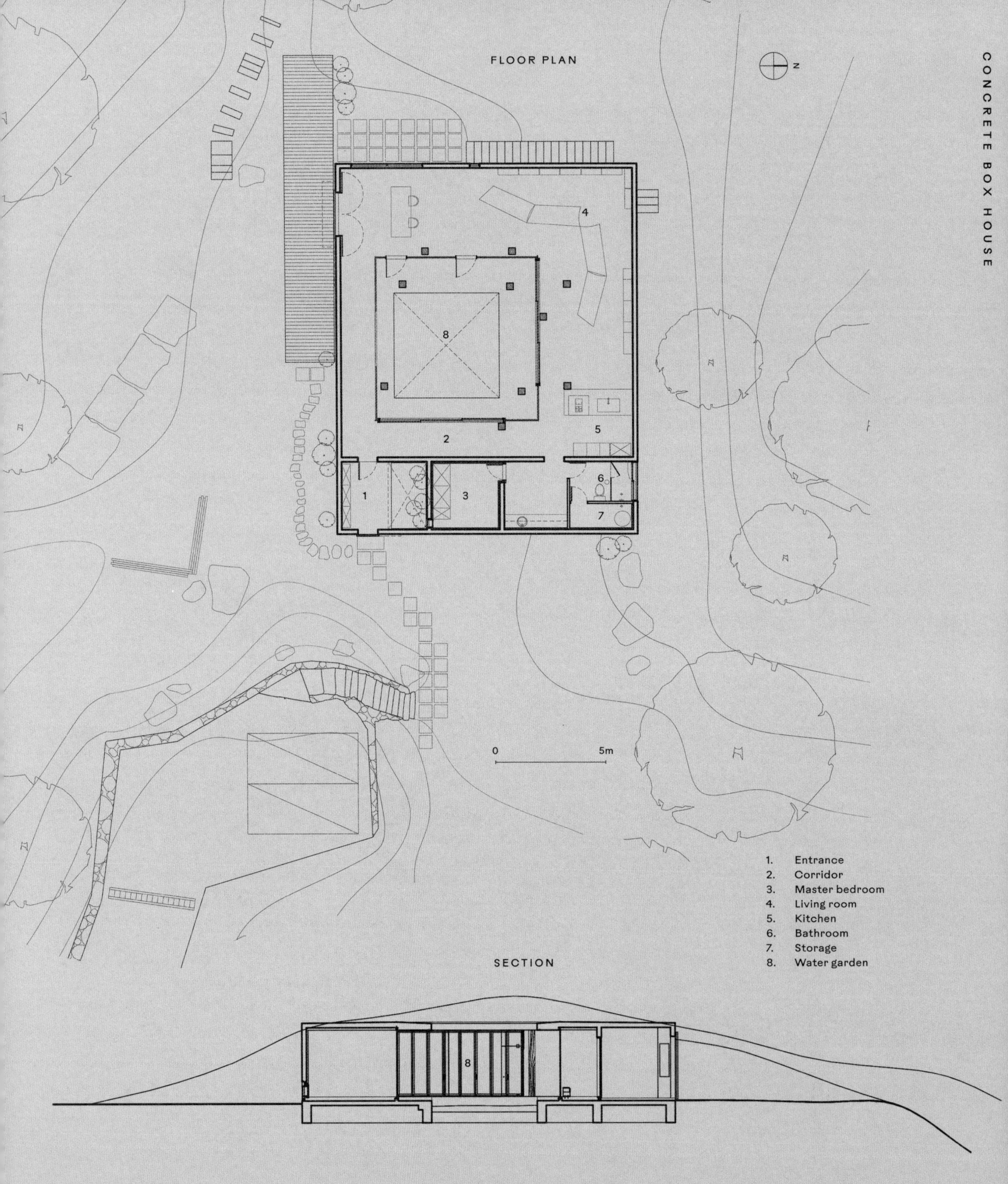

1. Entrance
2. Corridor
3. Master bedroom
4. Living room
5. Kitchen
6. Bathroom
7. Storage
8. Water garden

This is a square space, measuring 13.4 × 13.4 m (44 × 44 ft). If Earth House is a box embedded within the earth, Concrete Box House is a box placed on top of it. Although the square-box shape may appear imposing and impenetrable from the outside, once inside there is a sense of entering a space that expands to encompass the natural surroundings. The instinct to wander, opening up endless possibilities, ultimately leads to a feeling of completion. Within this expansive space, free of beams and columns, I have erected ten wooden pillars. Placing these ancient pieces of wood in their appropriate locations adds a dynamic dimension to the square living room/dining space that surrounds the inner courtyard, suggesting a natural flow in the overall movement through the building.

What do we mean when we say 'natural'? It is an ambiguous term. Perhaps it is closest to 'suitable' in meaning. In my opinion, it can be defined as the beauty found in the empty spaces of things left unfinished. Or perhaps it is the absence created by the application of restraint. In my projects, I often use the form of a box with straight lines – not only because it is an easy shape to work with in drawings and construction, but also because it combines simplicity with the potential for diverse and varied interior experiences. A simple space is one without any special architectural features, shaped into the most basic form of a box and furnished with only the essentials. This is the architecture of air, moonlight and earth, where it is enough for the space to be somewhere one may commune with nature.

The inner courtyard measures 7.4 × 7.4 m (24 ft 3 in. × 24 ft 3 in.) window to window. In this space, which is open to the earth below and the sky above, I created a pond of the same size as the opening to reflect the sky, the earth, the stars and the wind. The pond naturally refills and purifies water through a process of drawing up subterranean water and then allowing it to sink back slowly into the ground to begin the cycle again. The purity of building with the fewest materials is crucial, but by using rubbed concrete for insulation, placing glass directly into the concrete rather than having a metal frame, reducing the amount of concrete poured, and applying various other experimental techniques, the building becomes concise as well as environmentally friendly.

The experience of looking up at the trees and the clear sky through the opening, from a depth of 2.4 m (7 ft 10 in.), and the experience of looking down into the earth from the roof of Concrete Box House offer very different impressions. This difference in sensation is not simply visual, but one of physical placement, which suggests a subtle distinction between physical exploration and perception. In short, the experiential perception transcends visual understanding, offering instead a fundamental, instinctive quality of perception. It could be said that this presents the ultimate point of origin in sustainable architecture – the existence of the earth, light, wind and plant life, felt through the body, the nose, the ears and the skin. This experience prompts one to realize: this is both the starting point and the destination of sustainable architecture.

LOCATION
Sugok-ri,
Jipyeong-myeon,
Yangpyeong-gun,
Gyeonggi-do,
South Korea

GROSS FLOOR AREA
191.14 m² (2,057 sq. ft)

STRUCTURE
Reinforced concrete,
wood, wood-patterned
exposed concrete

The entrance (above left and opposite) and back of the house (left).

ABOVE AND OPPOSITE
The south façade and the view from the living room.

OVERLEAF
(above) The inner courtyard from the roof; (below) Light filters from the courtyard into the living room.

BELOW AND OPPOSITE
Details of the roof, with a light dusting of snow, and the inner courtyard. The stones are used as seats.

OVERLEAF
Ten wooden pillars, reclaimed from old *hanoks*, add a dynamic dimension to the open courtyard and interior spaces.

PP. 48–49
Light from the inner courtyard illuminates the surrounding trees.

T W O B O X H O U S E

2 0 0 5

FIRST FLOOR PLAN

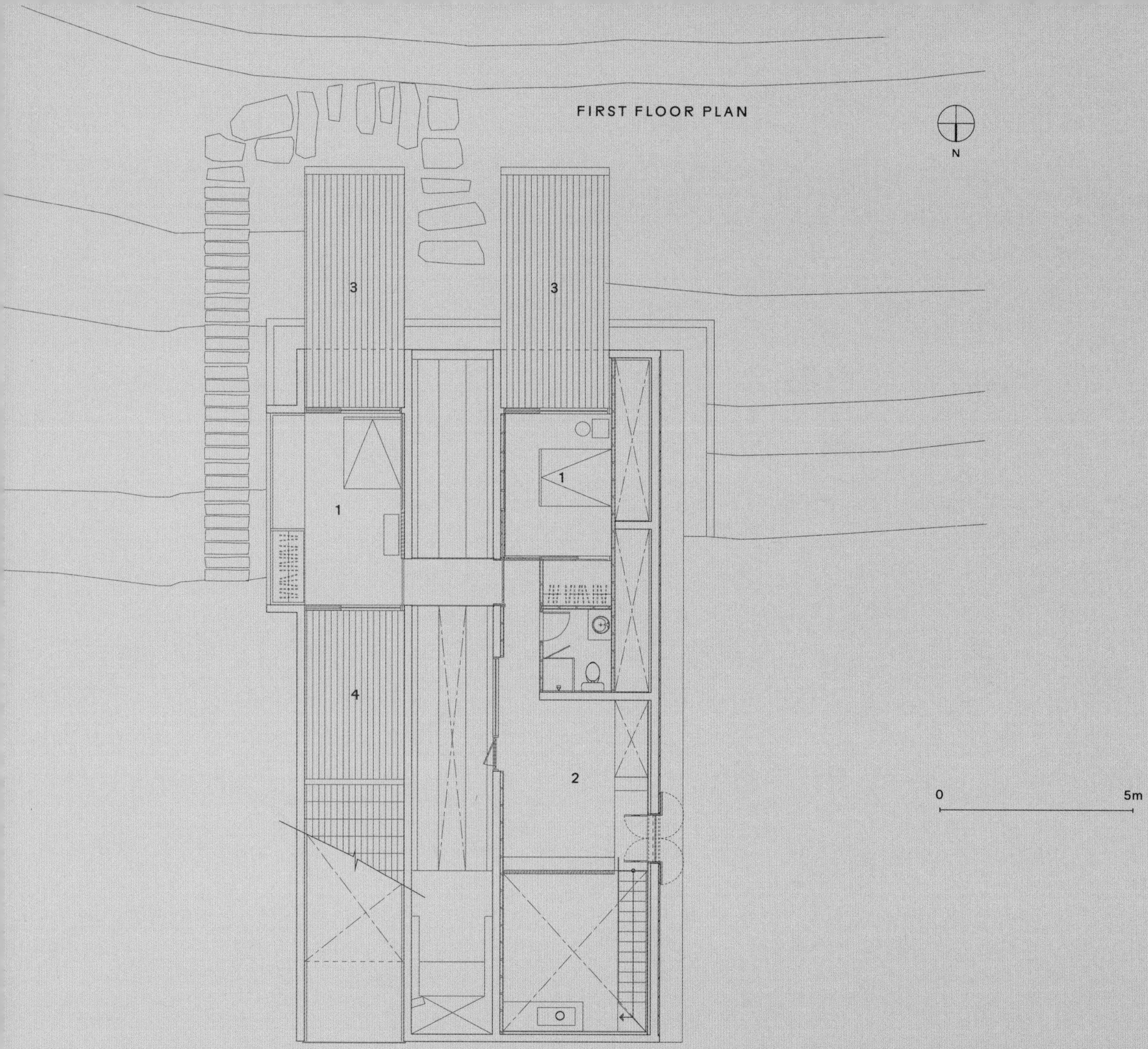

N

0 5m

1. Bedroom
2. Studio
3. Terrace
4. Sky space
5. Dining room
6. Kitchen
7. Multi-use room
8. Storage

SECTION

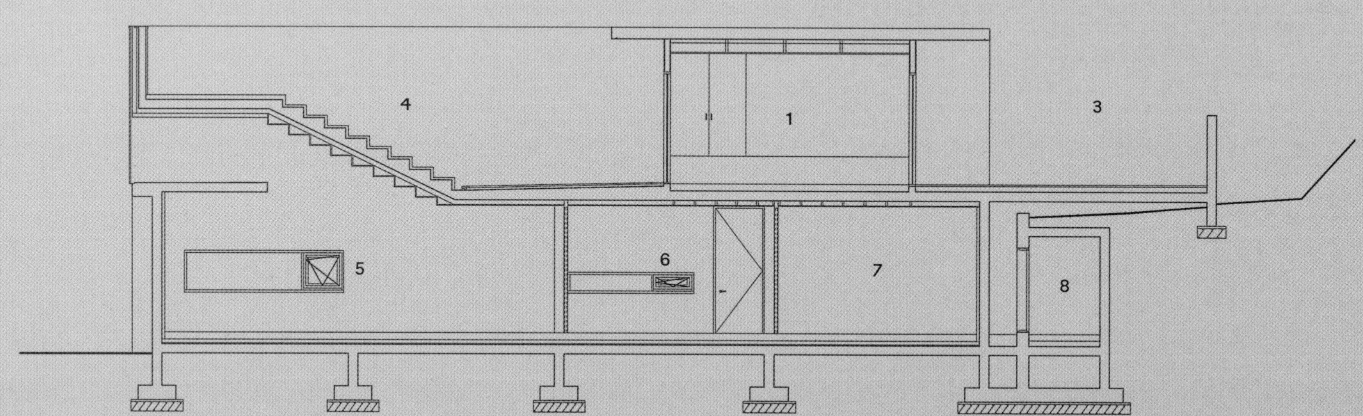

Two-Box House draws on the exploration of division and separation that I first developed in the Stone Wall House (2004). In this act of splitting, a tension arises – one that brings both cohesion and contrast to the spaces, allowing architecture to become a vessel for expressing the forces that connect and distinguish the inhabitants. Through this intentional tension, the experience of space and phenomena can become deeply heightened and profoundly felt.

The two-storey house is located on a hillside in Heyri Art Valley, a creative hub northwest of Seoul, where artists live, work and sell their art. It consists of two distinct structures of different sizes, which are separated by a 2.1-metre-wide (7-ft) courtyard and connected by a short bridge. The larger volume contains the main living room and a studio, as well as bedrooms and private quarters, all orientated towards the central courtyard. The smaller structure houses the kitchen and dining area on the ground floor and a bedroom above, as well as providing rooftop access to the surrounding landscape. The bridge unites the two volumes visually while maintaining a clear division between living and working spaces.

The house responds directly to the site's natural conditions, closely following the site plan while adapting to the existing topography. The result is a fluid link between the level changes, with the roof level corresponding to the top of the hill.

To encourage a deeper interaction with nature, all rooms enjoy views of a tranquil garden that has been created in the courtyard. The smaller building is punctuated at roof level to incorporate the hillside into the design, providing a space for inhabitants to observe the changing seasons. This space is crafted with a low parapet and a staircase that invites one to sit at roof level, immersed in the natural environment.

In the exterior, earthy red steel contrasts with exposed concrete, giving the building a rustic, grounded appearance, as well as hinting at an industrial influence. Frameless laminated skylights continue the premise of a rustic aesthetic, and the exposed reinforced concrete structure reveals the construction's raw, human touch. This choice to highlight the unrefined, essential materials speaks to the process of building itself, making the architecture both a reflection of its surroundings and a celebration of its making – an important concept in Korean aesthetics known as *mak*, meaning 'imperfection'. This word is pronounced *mahk*, which is my preferred spelling.

LOCATION
Beopheung-ri,
Tanhyeon-myeon,
Paju-si, Gyeonggi-do,
South Korea

GROSS FLOOR AREA
213.53 m^2 (2,298 sq. ft)

STRUCTURE
Reinforced concrete,
wood-patterned
exposed concrete,
steel plate with
specified paint finish

North façade, with
views of the entrance.

ABOVE
The southern façade and deck, seen from the dry garden.

OPPOSITE
The extruded kitchen window and a row of *onggi* vases along the western façade.

ABOVE
View of the first-floor bedrooms in the larger volume.

OPPOSITE
A bridge connects the first-floor bedroom in the smaller volume with the main living quarters.

ABOVE AND OPPOSITE
The living area, with a view of the courtyard between the two boxes.

OVERLEAF
A tranquil dry garden has been created in the courtyard, which can be seen from all the rooms.

L E E

O I

S O O

H O

U S E

2 0 0 6

FLOOR PLAN

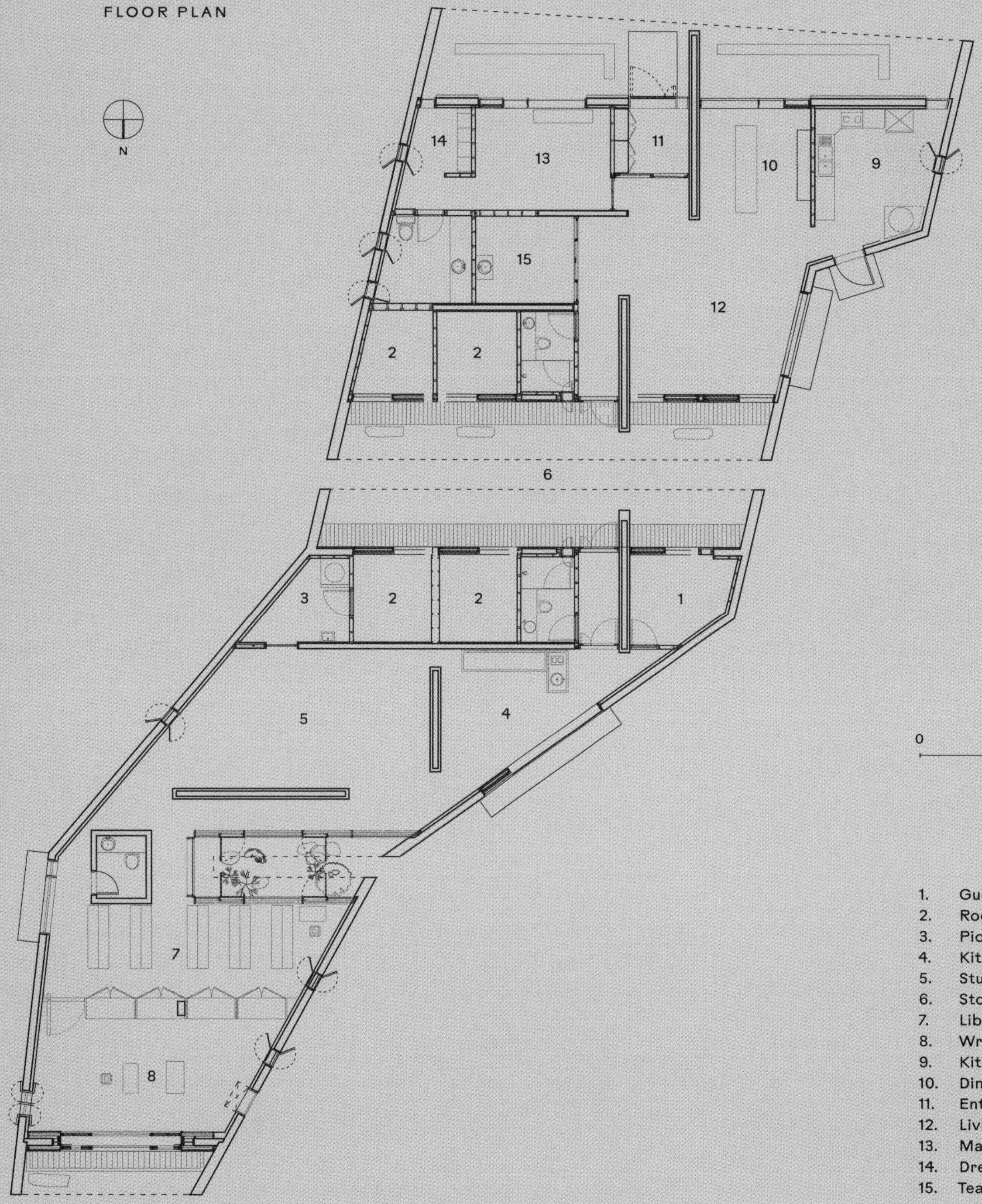

0 5m

1. Guest room
2. Room
3. Picture archive
4. Kitchenette
5. Studio
6. Stone garden
7. Library
8. Writing room
9. Kitchen
10. Dining room
11. Entrance
12. Living room
13. Master bedroom
14. Dressing room
15. Tea room

SECTION

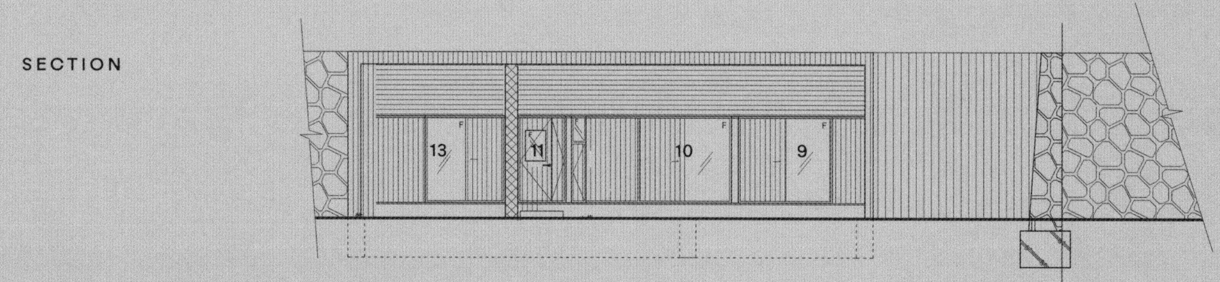

I always thought that the West too often took a hierarchical approach to nature, with man as the dominant force, continually attempting to tame and control the natural environment. The opposite is true of Korea, where man is considered as part of the natural environment. You can see this in landscape painting, where there is a particular emphasis on the harmonious relationship between architecture and its surroundings. The Lee Oisoo House (also known as the Fish-Shaped House) celebrates this idea, both becoming a harmonious fixture of the landscape and evoking a scene from a traditional painting.

Tucked away in a secluded spot surrounded by low hills, in an area known for its extraordinary scenery, the house has an especially rich and picturesque setting. Crystal-clear waters run through the long valley along the east–west axis and this flow of energy has influenced the design. I hoped to focus on retaining these unique elements and creating a house that could sufficiently absorb the unspoilt natural environment.

The house was designed for Oisoo Lee, a renowned writer and Zen painter who passed away in 2022, and reflects his maturity and image as a novelist and artist. The simple elements have been highlighted as much as possible to create a space where he could work in harmony with nature. Used by Lee and his wife predominantly for writing and painting, the house consists of two adjoining single-storey buildings that provide a divide between living and studio/working quarters. The living quarters consist mainly of a master bedroom, private living room and kitchen. The adjoining building to the north, with a narrow, crevice-like garden in between, houses a studio, kitchenette and guest room. Then there is another pocket garden, with the northern tip of the building featuring a writing room and library. Inspired by Lee's passion for the moon and his deep regard for nature, the living space receives natural light through voids planted with small gardens; they are also a vantage point where the couple could observe the ever-changing skies.

LOCATION
Damok-ri,
Sangseo-myeon,
Hwacheon-gun,
Gangwon-do,
South Korea

GROSS FLOOR AREA
273.29 m² (2,942 sq. ft)

STRUCTURE
Reinforced concrete,
exposed concrete finish

Views of the house from the north (left) and west (overleaf).

The living space (above) and the entrance to the house (opposite), facing south.

THIS PAGE AND OPPOSITE
The kitchenette (top left), living room (left) and studio (opposite).

PP. 86–87
The living room, with a view of the stone garden.

COMMUNITY

HOUSE

2008

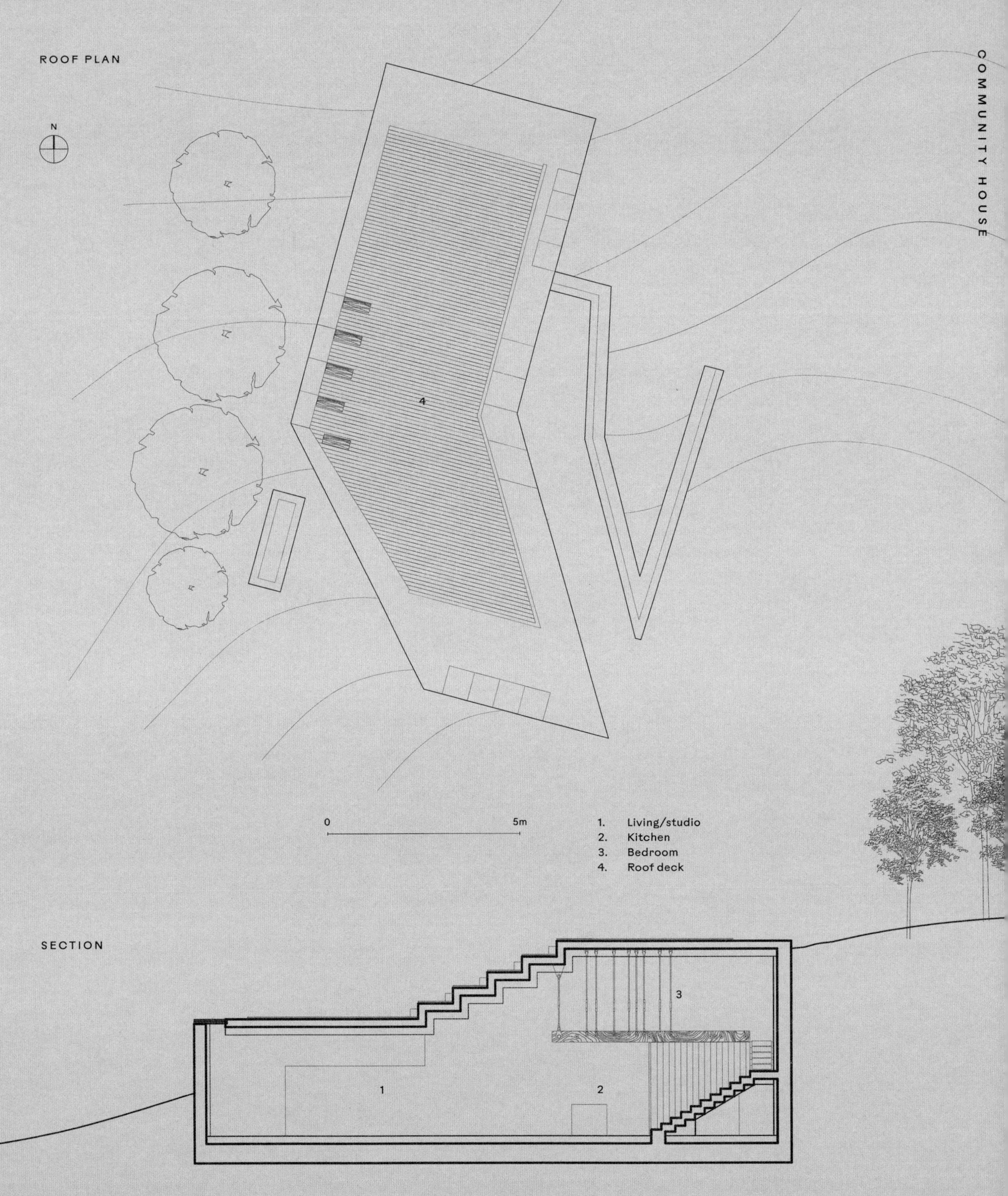
ROOF PLAN
N
4
0
5m
1. Living/studio
2. Kitchen
3. Bedroom
4. Roof deck
SECTION
1
2
3

Traditional Korean architecture responds viscerally to site conditions, following the mountains and the valleys. It shifts and twists as it navigates the landscape.

Nestled in dense woodland about an hour's drive from Seoul, Sugok-ri Community House is a large open-plan space where the local community can come together for social gatherings. Following the contours of the land, I intended the building's stepped roof to emerge from the ground and visually unite the levels, as well as functioning as a large outdoor meeting space. Facing the entrance to the complex, the structure acts as a threshold. I wanted its form to feel sculpted from the ground – deeply connected to the land – while allowing light to permeate both day and night. By day, sunlight filters into the recessed spaces through skylights; by night, light seeps outwards, softly illuminating the landscape.

As the site lacks open views in every direction and is surrounded by roads with passing vehicles, the approach I took was shaped by these conditions. Additionally, I wanted to create a space where residents could occasionally gather for activities like yoga or cooking, providing a more unique environment than a typical private house, while also offering a place to relax and socialize.

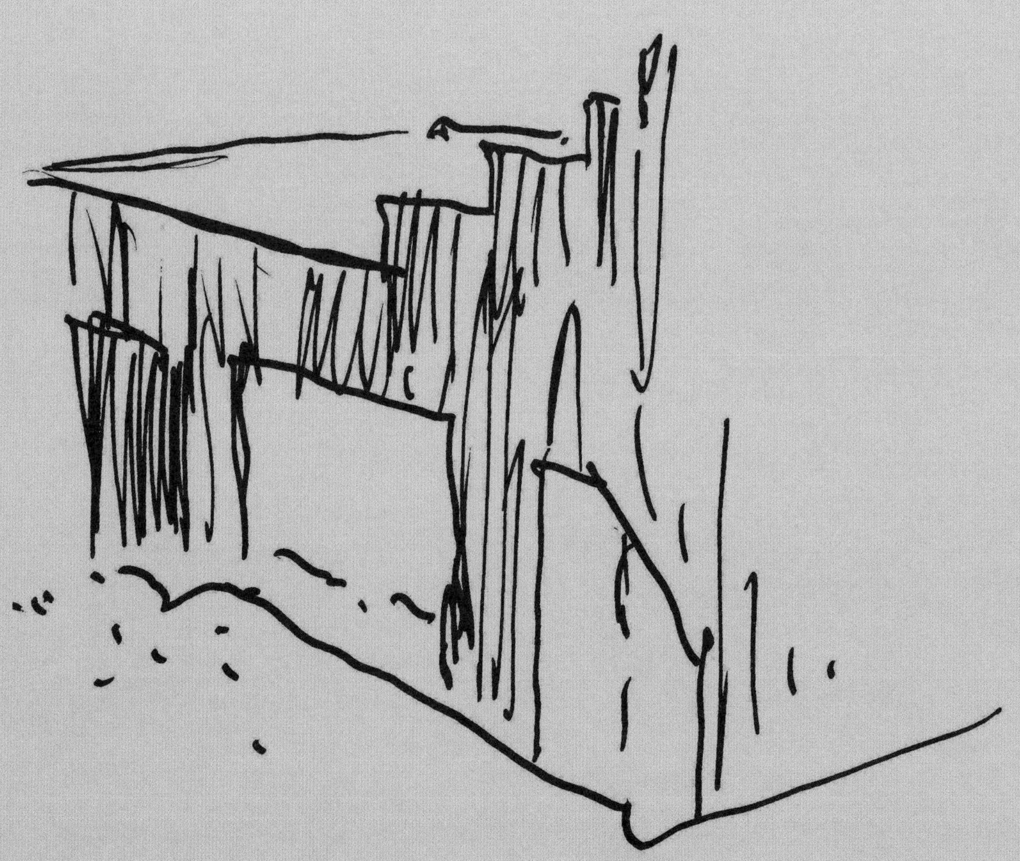

LOCATION
Sugok-ri,
Jipyeong-myeon,
Yangpyeong-gun,
Gyeonggi-do,
South Korea

GROSS FLOOR AREA
123.46 m² (1,329 sq. ft)

STRUCTURE
Reinforced concrete,
exposed concrete finish

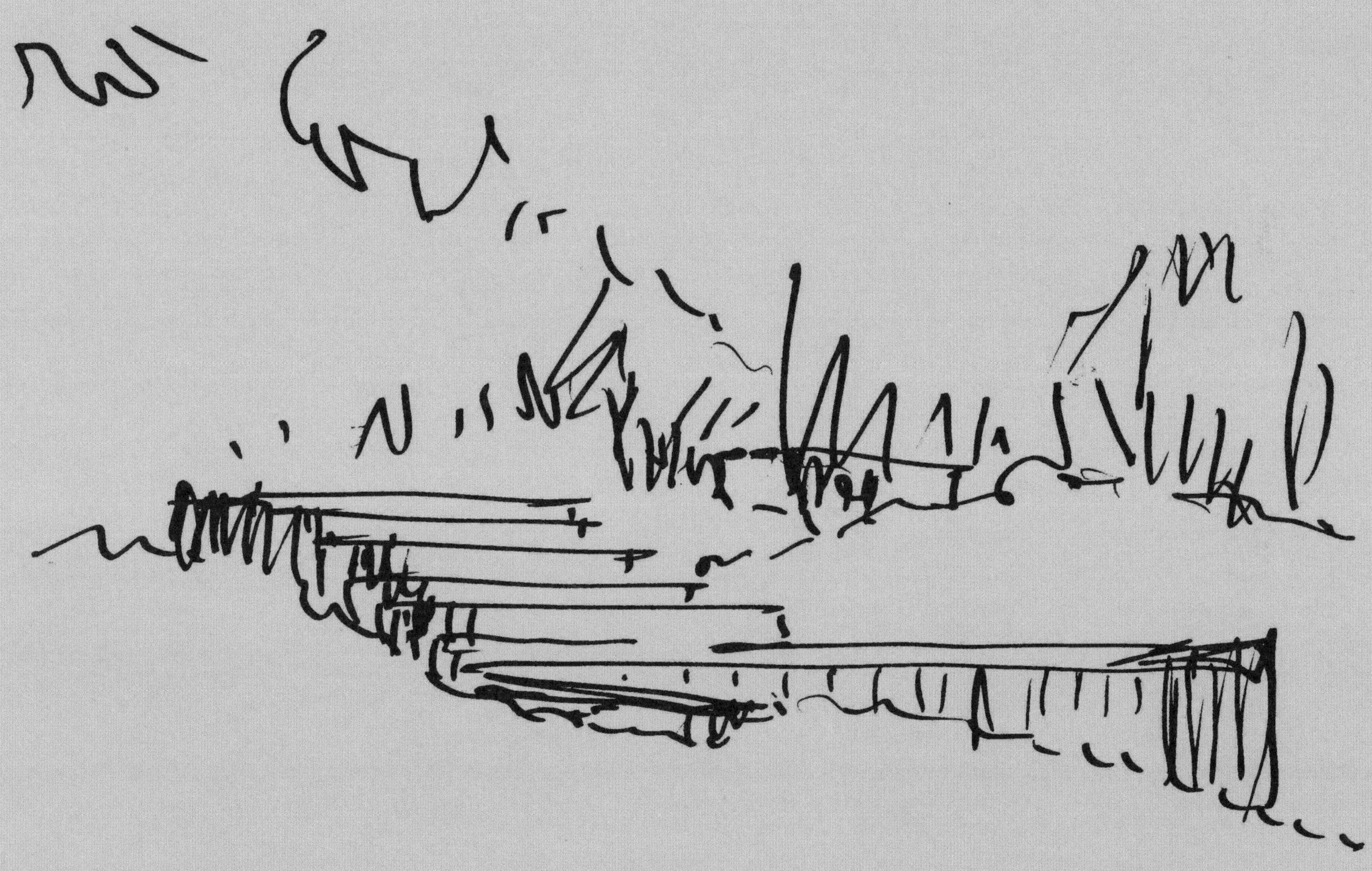

Embedded within the earth, the concrete structure attains high thermal mass and naturally moderates internal temperatures throughout the seasons. A concrete retaining wall extends the footprint, cutting into the ground to make space for the entrance. The concrete framework has been left exposed, with hollow construction ties, creating the impression of timber grain and giving texture to the exterior.

ABOVE
A concrete retaining wall cuts into the hillside, creating space for the entrance and a decked area.

OPPOSITE
The house from the west: the stepped roof doubles as an outdoor meeting area.

BELOW
The deck from the top of the retaining wall.

OPPOSITE
Light filters through skylights (above) into the versatile open-plan layout (below), seen here from the mezzanine.

P. 101
At night, artificial light streams through the skylights and illuminates the stepped roof.

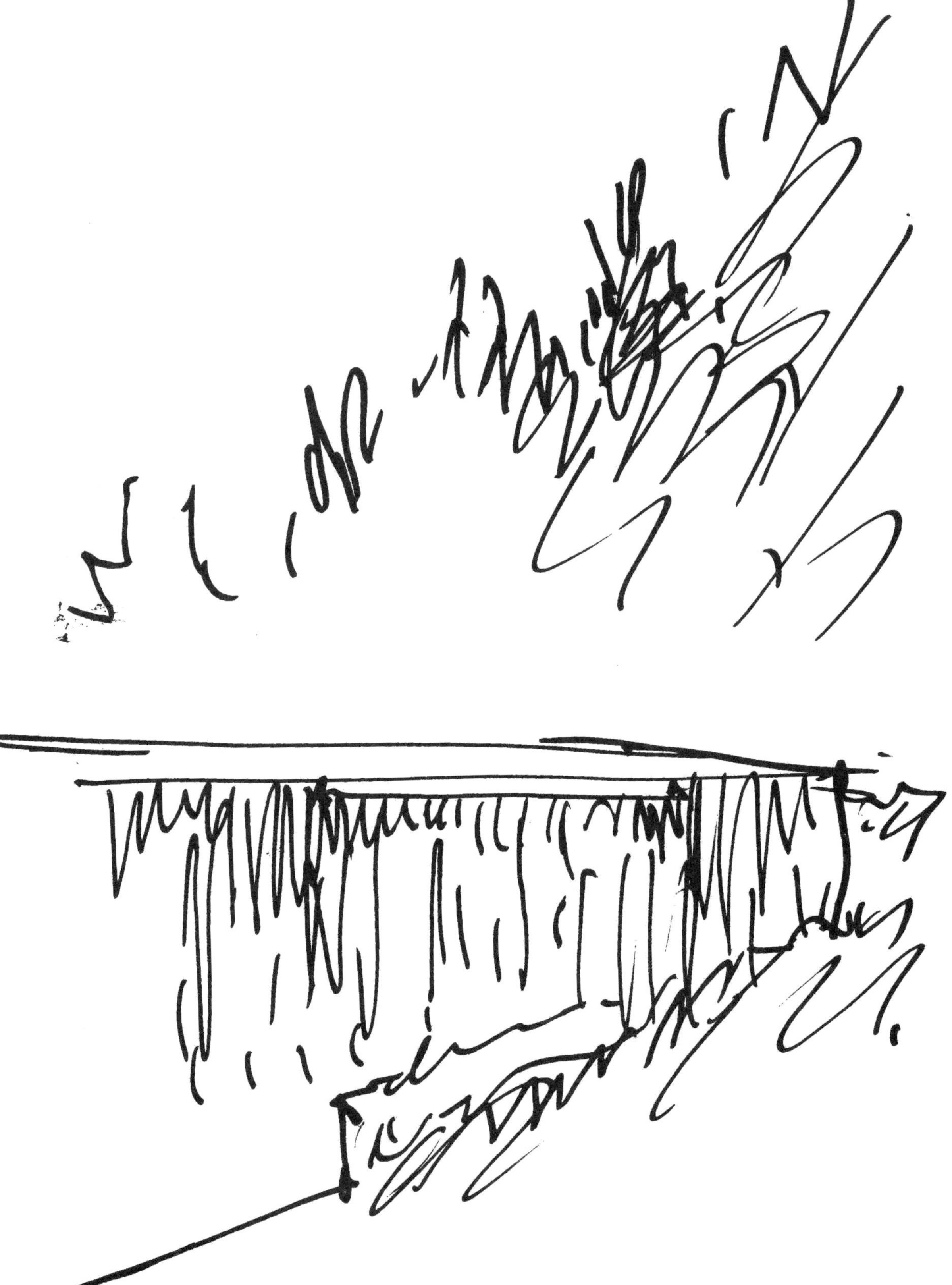

E A R T H H O U S E

2 0 0 9

FLOOR PLAN

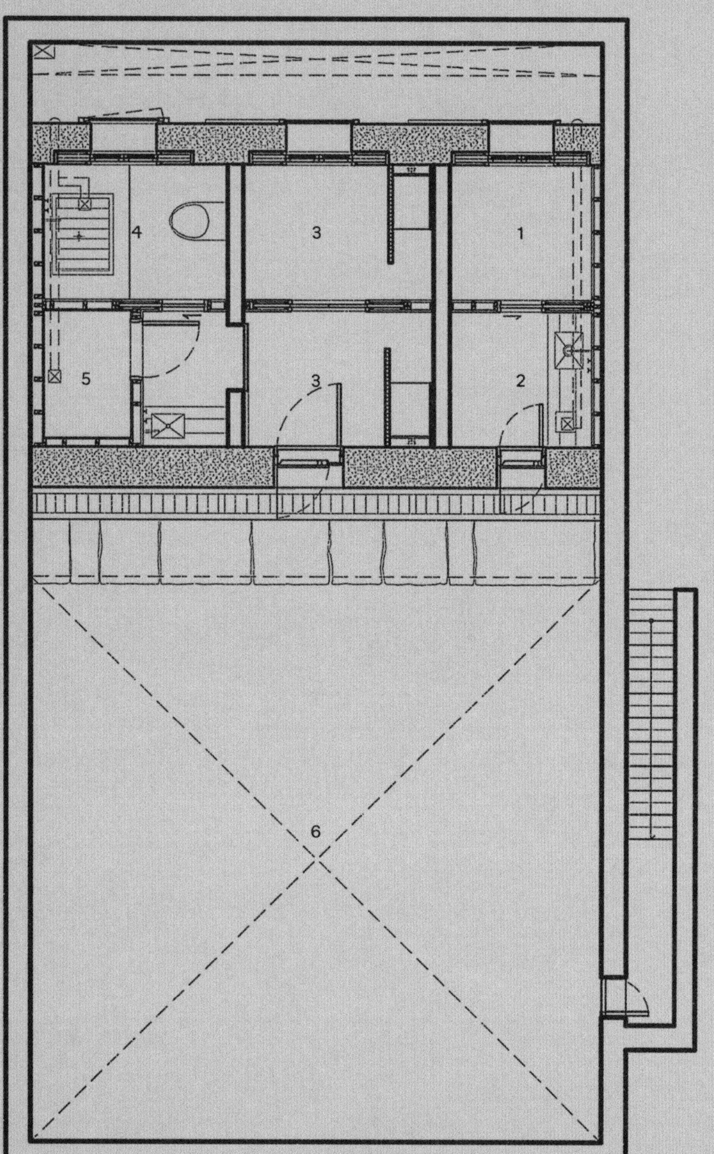

1. Study
2. Kitchen
3. Bedroom
4. Bathroom
5. Plant room
6. Courtyard

0 5m

SECTION

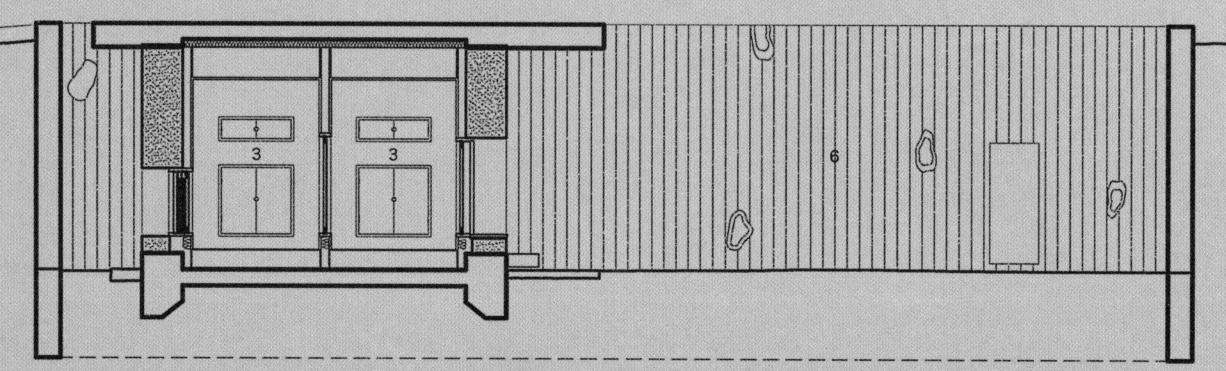

With its roof and land open to the halcyon sky, I also think of this house as the house of the sky. This project was built in homage to a poet I greatly admire, Dong-ju Yun, and his collection of poetry published posthumously in 1948 (later translated into English as *Sky, Wind, Stars and Poems*). It is, of all the projects developed from my graduate thesis, the simplest and most fundamental, embodying my thoughts about the earth in their purest form.

The straight, square space in the ground, where my friend's mother was finally laid to rest – a memory deeply embedded in my consciousness – is both a place of departure and a space in which life and hope can take root. Looking up at the endless sky from within the depths of the earth feels as comfortable, peaceful and calm as a mother's warm embrace. One might say that the instinctive desire to enter the earth is a fundamental human yearning for the safest and most nurturing place, to which we must return.

Dug into the ground, Earth House is composed of a small courtyard, made of reinforced concrete, and six rooms that are adjacent to one another: two bedrooms, a kitchen, a bathroom, a study and a plant room. Each room is one *pyeong* (about 3.3 m^2 or 36 sq. ft) in area, just big enough for an adult male to lie down with legs outstretched, but connecting rooms can be joined to make a bigger space. A narrow staircase is the only means of entry, with visitors accessing the courtyard through a prison-like grey steel door at the bottom of the stairs. The door is deliberately small, barely accommodating an adult, and some manoeuvring is required to squeeze through the opening.

Although the narrow steel door might initially evoke feelings of detachment and isolation, the experience of being inside the house is one of expansiveness and hope. The focus is on how nature should be experienced and received, as well as the perceptions and encounters that humans have within the natural world. This is a home sunken into the earth; yet from it, the experience is of the sky. This impression is most vivid when looking up at the sky from within the house – the house itself framing the waxing and waning of the moon, the movement of the wind, and the swaying branches of trees.

With the exception of the outer retaining walls, which are made of concrete, the entire structure – including the front and rear façades, as well as all interior partitions – is constructed from rammed earth excavated directly from the site. Within the 35 cm-thick (13¾ in.) concrete courtyard walls, wood from a pine tree that grew on the site has been inserted to decay over time. As the wood decays, fungi, grass and moss will grow, providing a fertile place for airborne seeds to take root. For this house, the goal is not completion but process. My hope is that it becomes a repository for beautiful memories, encouraging the ongoing processes of experience and perception that occur in everyday life.

Just as Yun's poems look to the future with hope, born from a time of struggle and urgency, and just as he sought to create hope through self-restraint and introspection, I also hoped this house could become a place to reflect on the 'we' of this generation. In making a deep well beside Earth House, I thought of Yun's poem 'Self-Portrait', in which the subject gazes at his reflection in a well, moved by pity and sorrow, and keeps returning to that reflection.

LOCATION
Sugok-ri,
Jipyeong-myeon,
Yangpyeong-gun,
Gyeonggi-do,
South Korea

GROSS FLOOR AREA
32.49 m² (350 sq. ft)

STRUCTURE
Reinforced concrete flat slab, wood-patterned exposed concrete, rammed earth

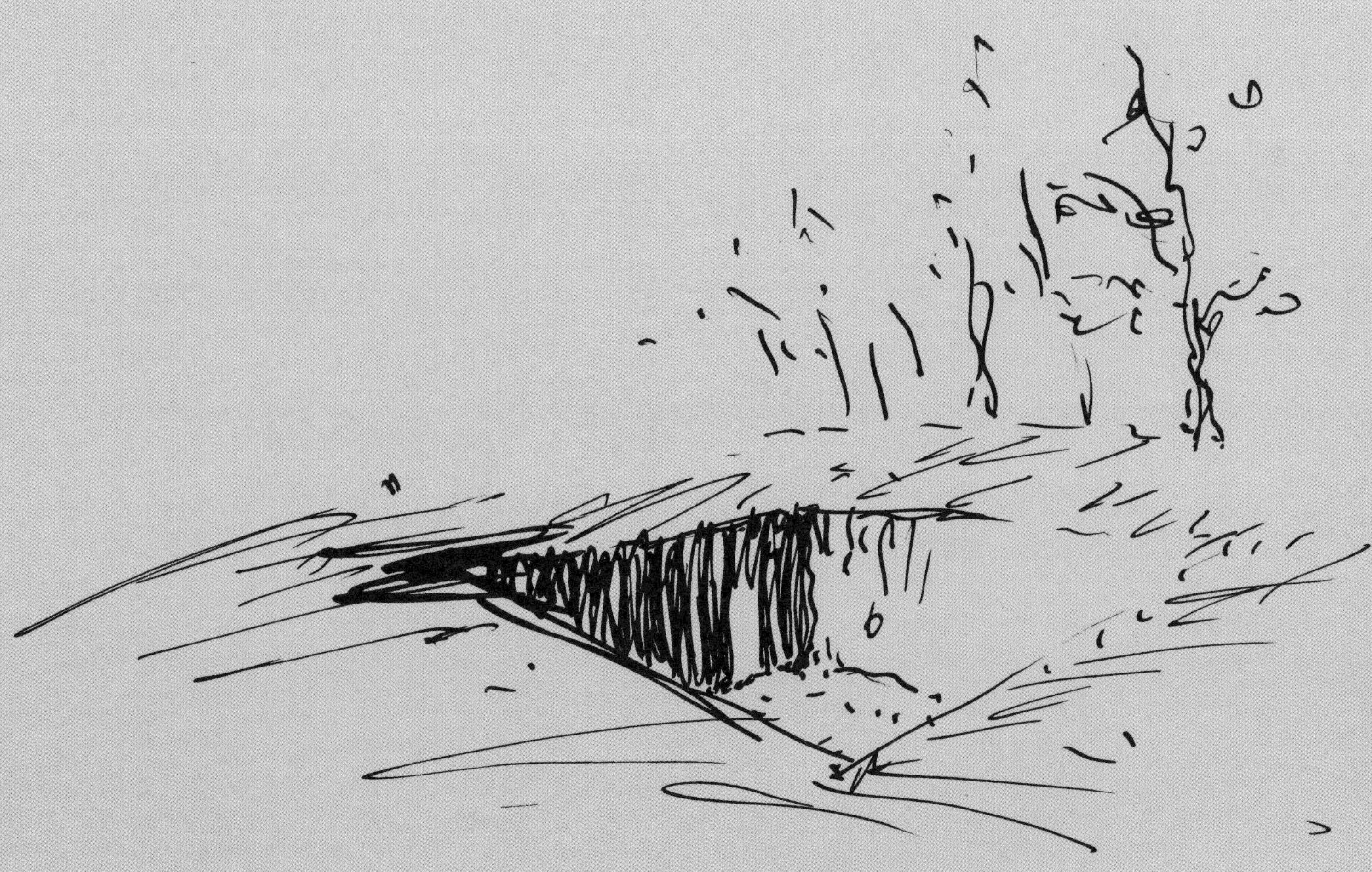

The embedded courtyard from ground level.

BELOW
A deep well, inspired by the poetry of Dong-ju Yun, becomes a place for reflection.

OPPOSITE
A narrow staircase, in the foreground, is the only means of entry.

Details of the steps (above),
made of upcycled wood, and the
concrete retaining wall (opposite)
from the top of the staircase.

LEFT
The grey steel door at the bottom of the stairs is deliberately small. Wood from a pine tree, designed to decay over time, is embedded in the concrete walls of the courtyard.

OVERLEAF
View from the courtyard into the house.

P. 119
A slither of courtyard at the back of the house creates space between the volume and the retaining wall.

PP. 120–21
Night-time view of the house from ground level, with light filtering through the narrow courtyard at the back of the house.

IN-EARTH MEDITATION HOUSE

2010

0 5m

1. Exterior deck
2. Meditation room
3. Entrance
4. Water garden
5. Bathroom

SECTION

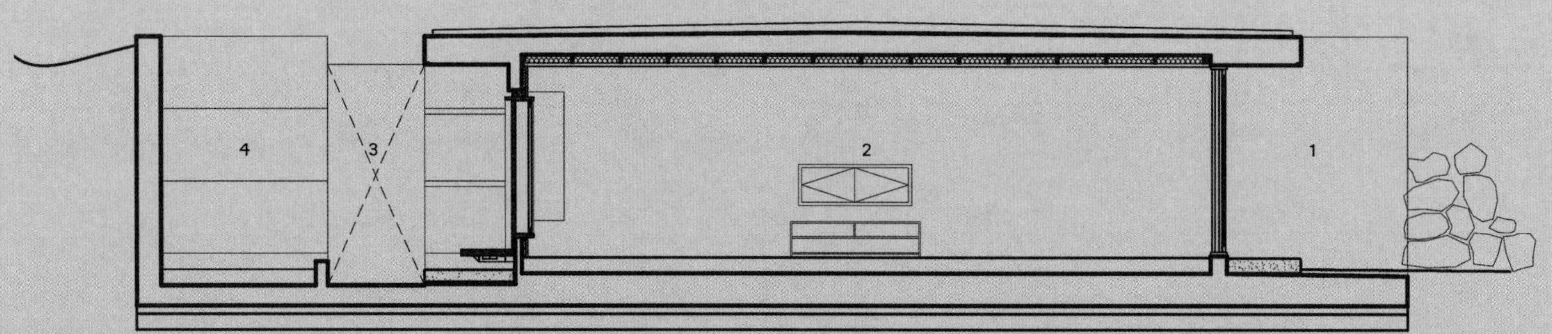

FLOOR PLAN

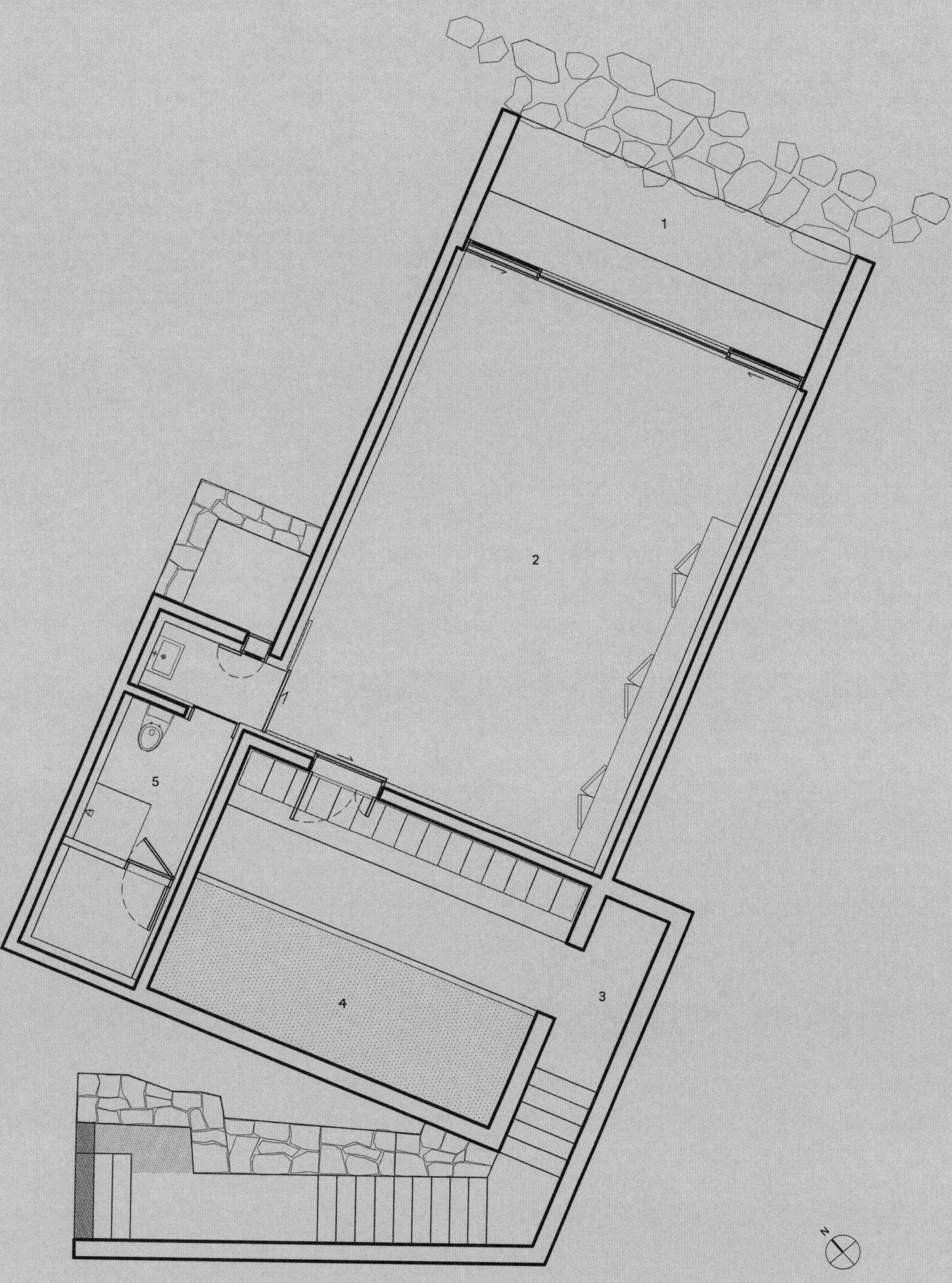

I believe that the main role of architecture is to unite – to enhance the experience of light and air, to connect us to our surroundings, to unlock emotions and metaphysical sensations. Architecture, to me, is about creating harmony, devising a sacred bond without extraneous detail or built-in distractions. Therefore, architecture should not be reactive to nature or distort it, but instead be receptive and offer an open experience of nature through minimal interventions.

Located on Jeju, Korea's largest island, In-Earth Meditation House lies in a peaceful spot characterized by gentle sea breezes and rolling hills. It is one of three square-shaped buildings I designed for the site, each carefully arranged in balance with the surrounding area.

In-Earth Meditation House is a square firmly embedded in the earth. The approach, a long staircase that leads to an exterior courtyard, emphasizes the profound symbolism of descending into the earth while at the same time creating a sense of anticipation – of the experience to come. The courtyard connects the interior of the building with nature, enabling a communion between nature and man. Visitors enter a sparsely furnished room with only the simplest of touches. The floor extends to sliding doors that open out to a terrace and the forest beyond, bringing a feeling of seclusion, serenity and belonging to the space.

LOCATION
Gyorae-ri,
Jocheon-eup,
Jeju-si, Jeju-do,
South Korea

GROSS FLOOR AREA
60 m² (646 sq. ft)

STRUCTURE
Reinforced concrete,
exposed concrete finish

The embedded house, in the foreground, from ground level. The Jedong Ranch Dining Pavilion, also designed by Byoung Cho, can be seen in the background.

BELOW
A side window brings in additional light from the passageway.

OPPOSITE
A wooden canopy protects the interior of the building, which is accessed from a sunken courtyard.

BELOW
The house from the west, with its lawn-covered roof.

OPPOSITE
The sparsely furnished interior and the terrace, with views of the forest beyond.

SCISSORS HOUSE

2010

0 5m

1. Bedroom
2. Bathroom
3. Living room
4. Dining room
5. Kitchen
6. Support kitchen
7. Utility room
8. Courtyard
9. Master bedroom

SOUTH ELEVATION

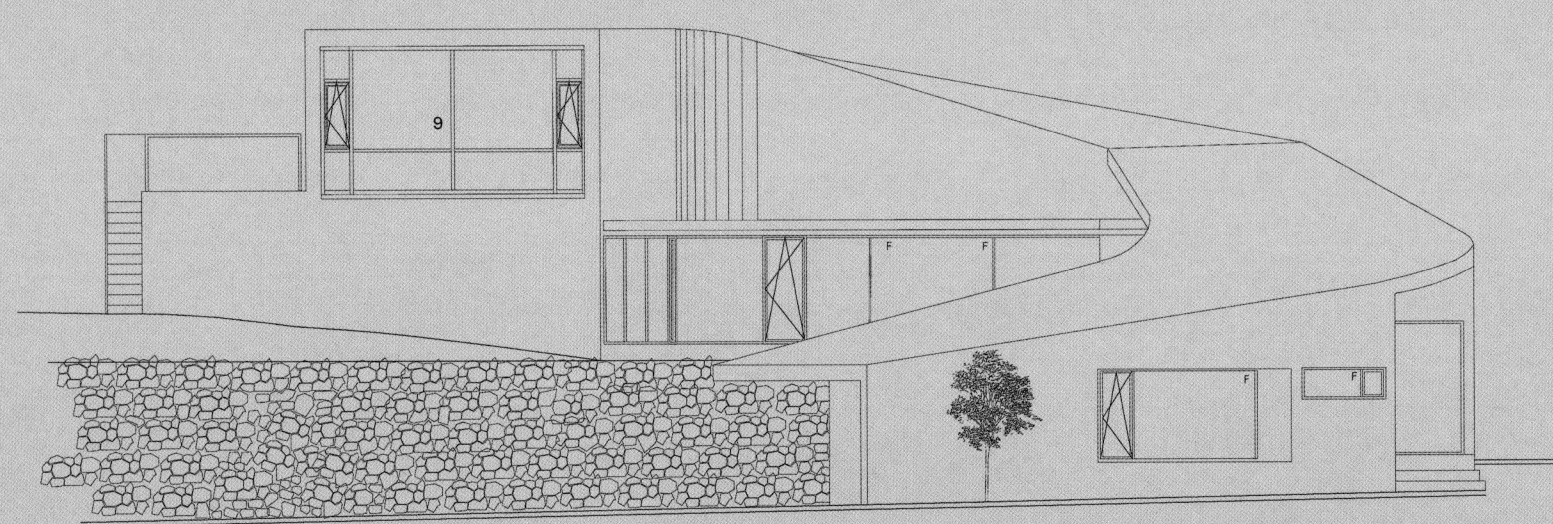

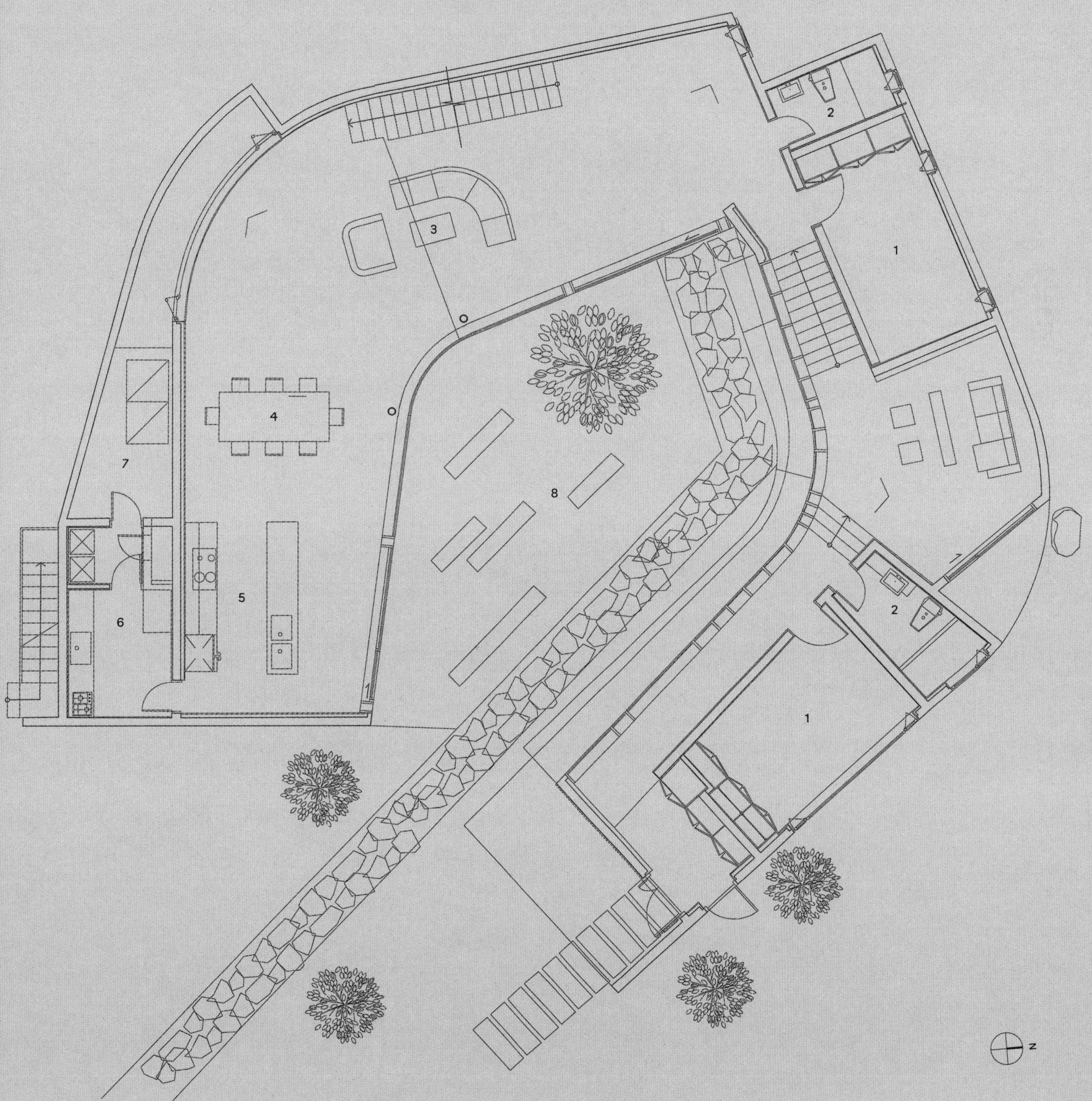
2
3
1
4
7
8
5
6
2
1
N

Too often, architecture ignores the profound poetic impression that the preservation of nature can instil. Rather than coalescing with the sublime, it becomes unsympathetic and hostile. Jeju inspires a deep reverence for the island's beauty: the changing winds, untouched hills, towering ridges and volcanic terrain – dominated by Hallasan, a volcano and Korea's tallest peak – particularly resonate with me.

Located on a steeply sloping site in the south of the island, Scissors House was designed and orientated to take full advantage of the natural conditions, while preserving much of the old tangerine farm on which it was built. The site is terraced and defined by 2–3-metre-high (6½–10 ft) agrarian retaining walls made of basalt – a volcanic rock that is abundant on the island – imbuing the landscape with a certain charm. I decided to keep these elements and design a building that responds to the existing features of the site.

The three-storey, split-level house takes its name from the way it 'scissors' between two tiers, stepping up and folding around a central stone wall. This formal decision compacts the design by pivoting the house on an axis, allowing for a small stone garden in the pocket of space that is created by the building's looping form.

From the entrance on the ground floor, the main part of the house is accessed by an angled staircase that wraps around the stone garden. Expansive windows in the living area open up the interior to a courtyard and views of the Pacific Ocean beyond, creating a sense of seamless connection between the indoors and outdoors. A mezzanine level directly above the kitchen and dining area becomes a spacious en-suite bedroom.

To take advantage of the Pacific breeze, while still remaining sheltered from the strong tropical winds, the house is orientated towards the ocean with a low and continuous roof form. To ensure that the monolithic roof survives the typhoon-prone environment, the single slab of concrete was re-trowelled every 2–3 hours, keeping the structure completely watertight.

LOCATION
Seohong-dong, Seogwipo-si, Jeju-do, South Korea

GROSS FLOOR AREA
322.3 m^2 (3,469 sq. ft)

STRUCTURE
Reinforced concrete, exposed concrete finish

BELOW AND OVERLEAF
A staircase curves up from the entrance (below) to the main part of the house, wrapping around a stone garden.

PP. 148–49
(left) Stairs lead from the living room to a mezzanine, housing the master bedroom; (right) View of the garden from the living quarters.

BELOW AND OPPOSITE
The curved façade of the kitchen/dining area.

PP. 152–55
The sweeping roof responds to the existing site, a former tangerine farm defined by agrarian walls.

2010

L-SHAPED HOUSE

FLOOR PLAN

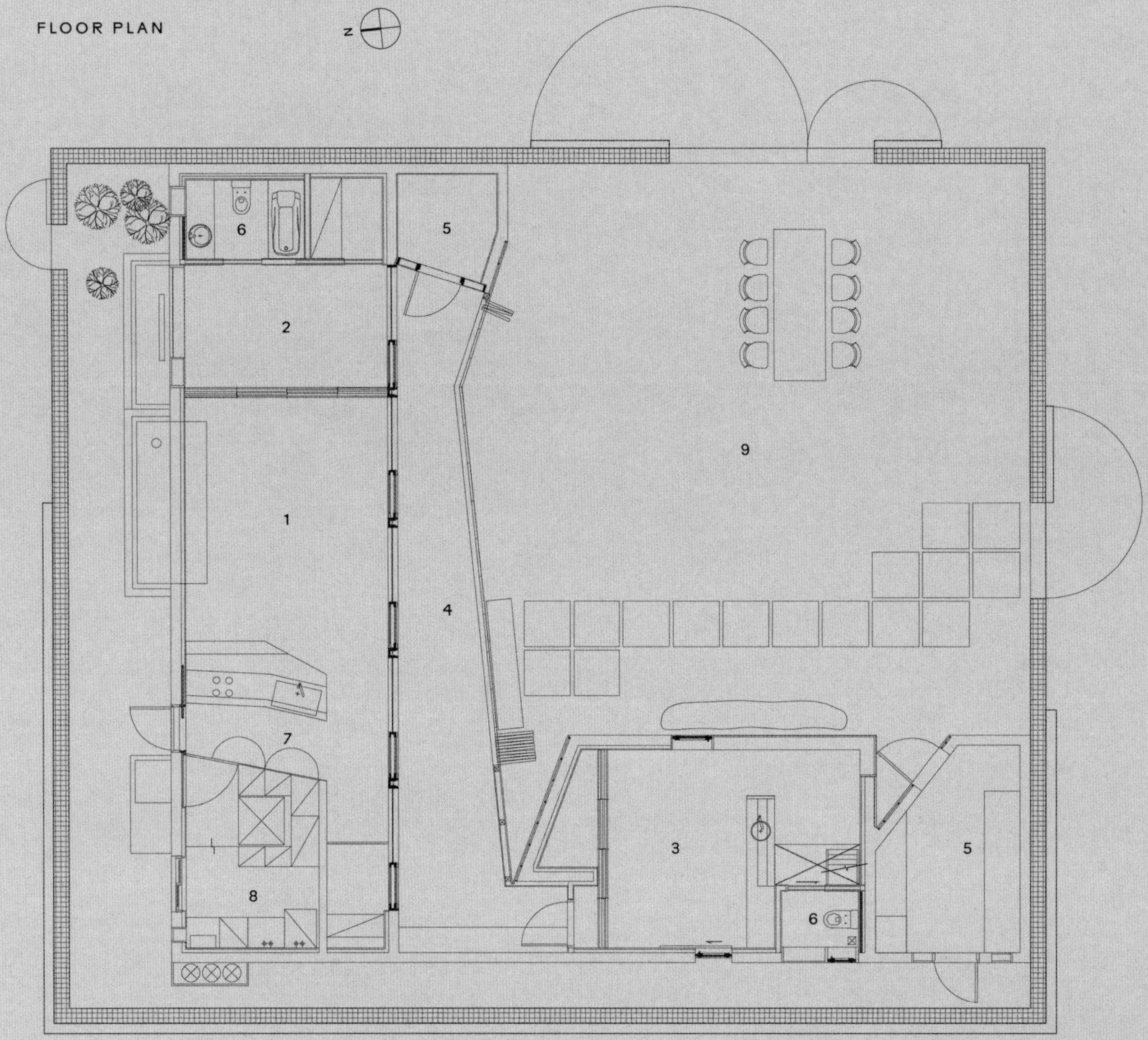

0 5m

1. Living room
2. Master bedroom
3. Guest room/Tea room
4. Terrace
5. Storage
6. Bathroom
7. Kitchen
8. Support kitchen
9. Courtyard

SECTION

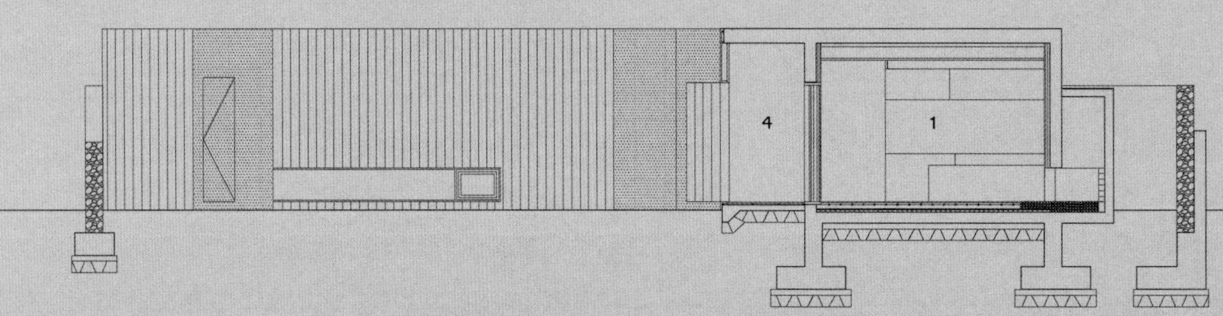

The L-Shaped House is a single-storey residence situated by a small mountain called Mount Bonghwa in an industrial area outside Seoul. Commissioned by a couple working in the capital, the house was designed to be both a weekend retreat and a future permanent home.

When the clients purchased the land, they acquired the adjacent property as well, which provided expansive views to the south and east. Initially, I envisioned the house as a square, orientated to embrace the surrounding trees and the mountains. However, I soon realized that an L-shaped layout would be more practical for creating private exterior spaces that take full advantage of the vistas. In addition, the L-shape works as a shield to block off any disturbance from the road on the west and enhance security of the entire property.

The house is designed with the couple's lifestyle in mind – both are early risers, so the principal sleeping area is positioned to capture the morning sunlight. I also incorporated natural cross-ventilation features, which help maintain a comfortable interior temperature, especially during the hot, humid summers when the house is most frequently in use.

The main living area is flexible, with the lounge and master bedroom divided by a movable wall system, connecting to a broad, covered deck to the south. The guest bedroom is separated by the covered deck, which is adjacent to the main living area. This shaded outdoor space acts as an intermediate area between the main interior space and the exterior courtyard. An accordion-like door system along the outer edge of the deck can be fully opened when the couple are at home and securely closed when the house is empty. The large overhang ensures that sunlight enters the living space only in the winter months, while keeping the interior cooler during the summer, when the sun appears higher in the sky.

At the heart of the L-shape is a courtyard, paved with locally sourced white basalt stone. This material was chosen specifically to reflect light back into the house, which features a long, low, continuous window that brings in natural light from the courtyard. The effect is subtle but effective, casting soft, indirect light into the interior to create a warm and inviting atmosphere. The use of pale woods and white surfaces further enhances this sense of calm, making the living space feel open and informal.

The courtyard itself is minimally landscaped, with a single planted tree anchoring one corner. This simple, low-maintenance design provides ample space for a range of activities, while the layout ensures that the home remains connected to the outdoors all year round.

LOCATION
Hwasan-ri,
Ujeong-eup,
Hwaseong-si,
Gyeonggi-do,
South Korea

GROSS FLOOR AREA
139.13 m² (1,498 sq. ft)

STRUCTURE
Reinforced concrete,
exposed concrete finish

THIS PAGE
The front of the house, seen here with the accordion-like door closed (above) and open (below).

OPPOSITE
The covered deck acts as an intermediate space between interior and exterior.

BELOW AND OPPOSITE
Detail of the concrete countertop (below) in the open-plan living room (opposite).

OVERLEAF
Exterior deck, with the entrance to the house on the right and a guest room, also used as a tea room, on the left.

P. 169
Views of the tea room: looking towards the entrance (above) and into the space (below). The ladder leads to a small attic/storage space.

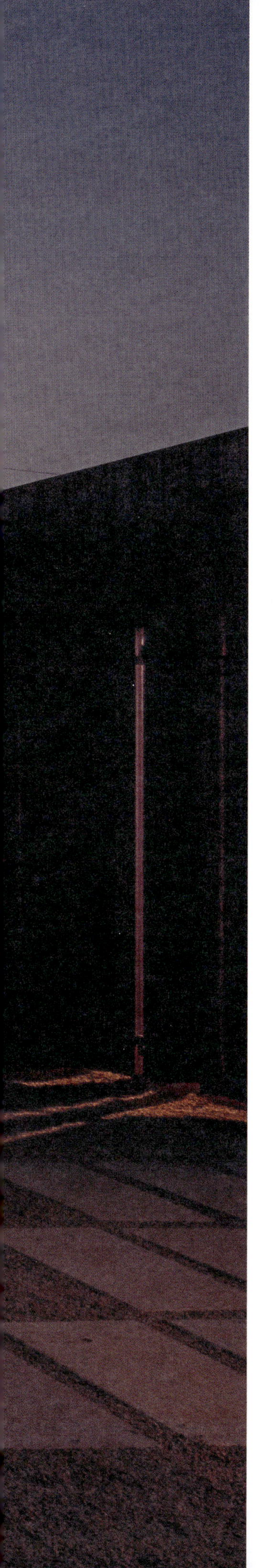

At night, light filters from the guest room through a long, low window into the courtyard (opposite) and from the kitchen/dining area (below).

T I L T
R O
O
F
H O
U S E

2
0
4 1

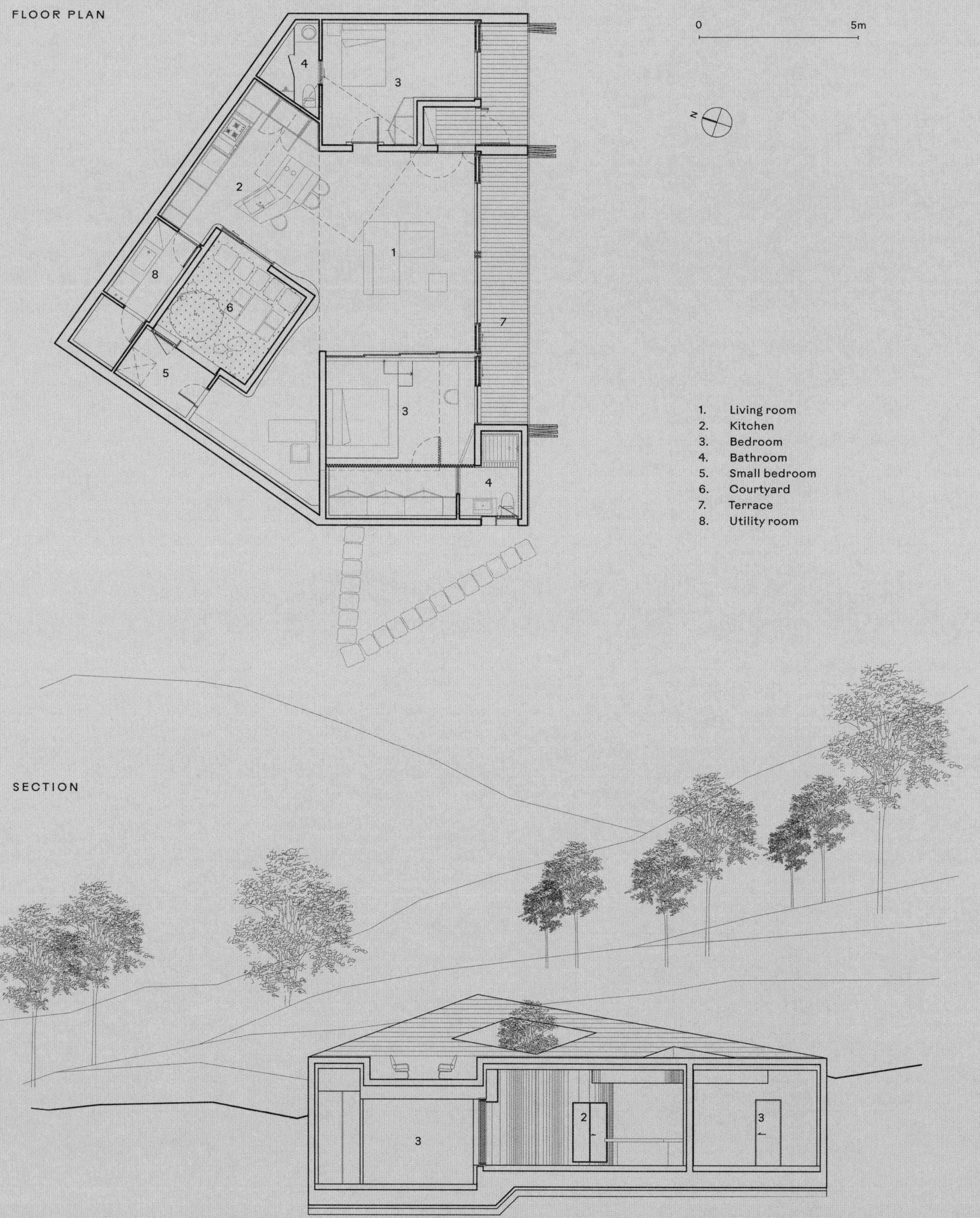
FLOOR PLAN
0
5m
N
1
2
3
3
4
4
5
6
7
8
1. Living room
2. Kitchen
3. Bedroom
4. Bathroom
5. Small bedroom
6. Courtyard
7. Terrace
8. Utility room
SECTION
2
3
3

When I first visited the site, I had to crawl up the hillside because it was so steep. It was a difficult experience, and I felt quite overwhelmed. I also wondered how I could design a house in such conditions. There wasn't even enough space to create a garden. This initial challenge became the starting point for the design itself. Rather than resisting the site, I chose to work with it – to let the topography define the form and logic of the house.

Overlooking a valley, the resulting structure is a compact, convex pentagon-shaped box, deeply embedded into the upper part of the hill. Its roof is tilted to follow the gradient of the hill, as well as being accessible, providing a viewing platform – with the house appearing to drop away almost, to disappear into the ground. Although the demanding conditions of the terrain required several changes to the plans, this house embodies my commitment to exploring the fundamentals of the relationship between the building and its surroundings. The unique shape of the house is the direct result of building in harmony with the Ki of nature, the universal energy that permeates through everything: the slope of the roof embraces the contours of the landscape, while the lower half of the house is flat and parallel to the road, enabling easy access.

This two-bedroom house has characteristics of Earth House and Concrete Box House. The roof is punctuated by three square-shaped, partially recessed 'boxes'. The two boxes at the front of the house are 70 cm (27½ in.) and 80 cm (31½ in.) in depth, respectively, and are intended as external seating areas – spaces in which to relax and enjoy the southern aspect of the mountains, the far line of the horizon or the stars in the night sky. The third box is cut into the house, extending from the roof to the ground floor to form an open courtyard.

The entire front elevation, including the large folding doors, is covered with smooth pine planks, which have been treated with black oil to protect them from the weather. The dark wood contrasts with the light and airy interior, with its large windows, white-painted walls and expanses of yellow birch. The recessed boxes on the roof help to define different areas internally, with lower ceiling heights creating an air of intimacy in the master bedroom and the kitchen. The living areas have higher ceilings and therefore a more spacious feel.

The embedded rear portion of the living space, occupied by the kitchen area, required cross-ventilation and natural light. The open courtyard was introduced as a crucial element to address the challenges of lighting and ventilation typically associated with underground spaces. It allows summer breezes from the south to enter naturally and exit, ensuring proper airflow and comfort.

LOCATION
Sugok-ri,
Jipyeong-myeon,
Yangpyeong-gun,
Gyeonggi-do,
South Korea

GROSS FLOOR AREA
161.78 m² (1,741 sq. ft)

STRUCTURE
Reinforced concrete,
exposed concrete finish

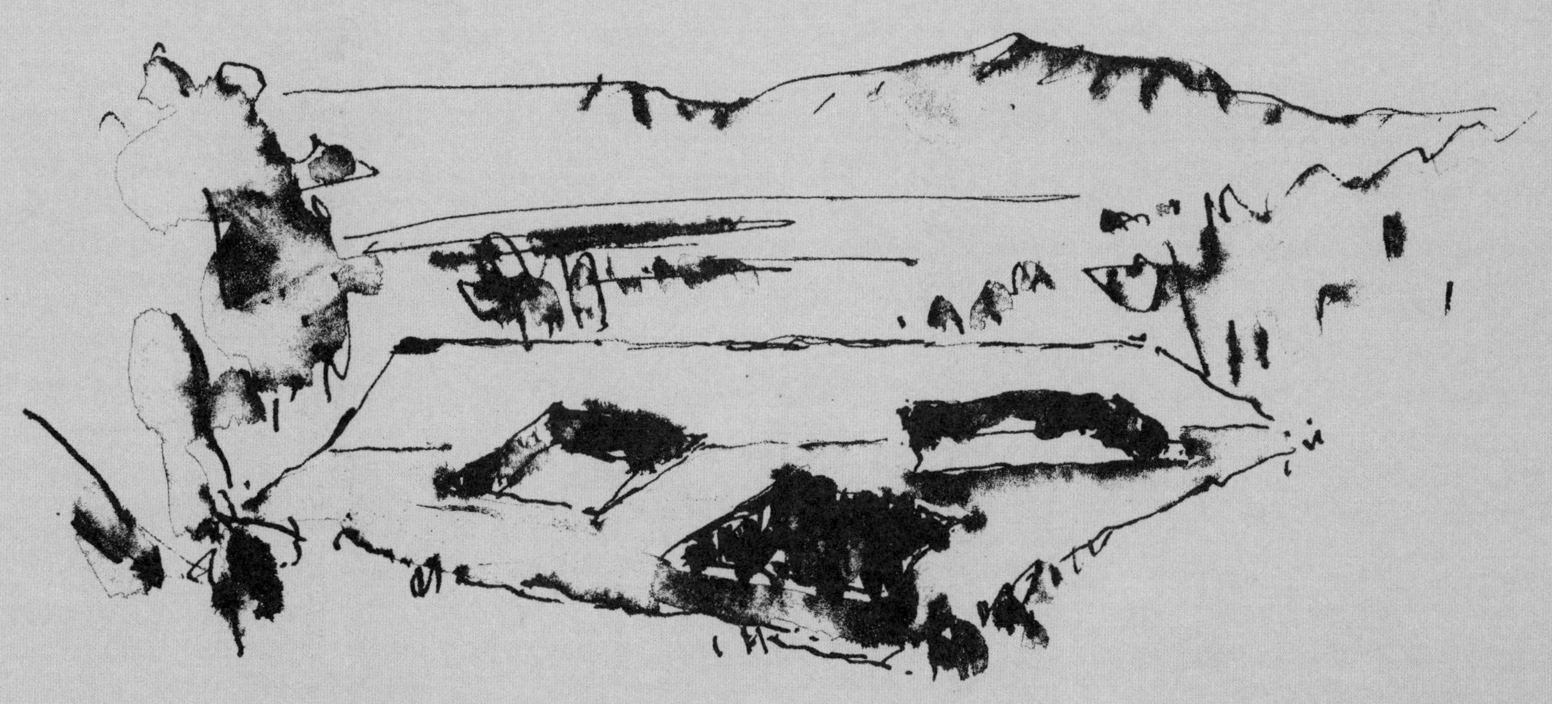

The front of the house: the façade is covered with pine that has been treated with black oil to protect it from the weather. Doors fold back to reveal a deck.

The view from the bedroom
into the kitchen (above),
and vice versa (opposite).

BELOW
The living room offers expansive views of rice fields and mountains.

OPPOSITE
Curved walls soften the interior, as well as providing spaces for contemplation.

BELOW
Steps at the side of the building provide access to the roof.

PP. 188–89
The roof features two recessed boxes with outdoor seating. A third box defines the inner courtyard, providing ventilation and light at the back of the house.

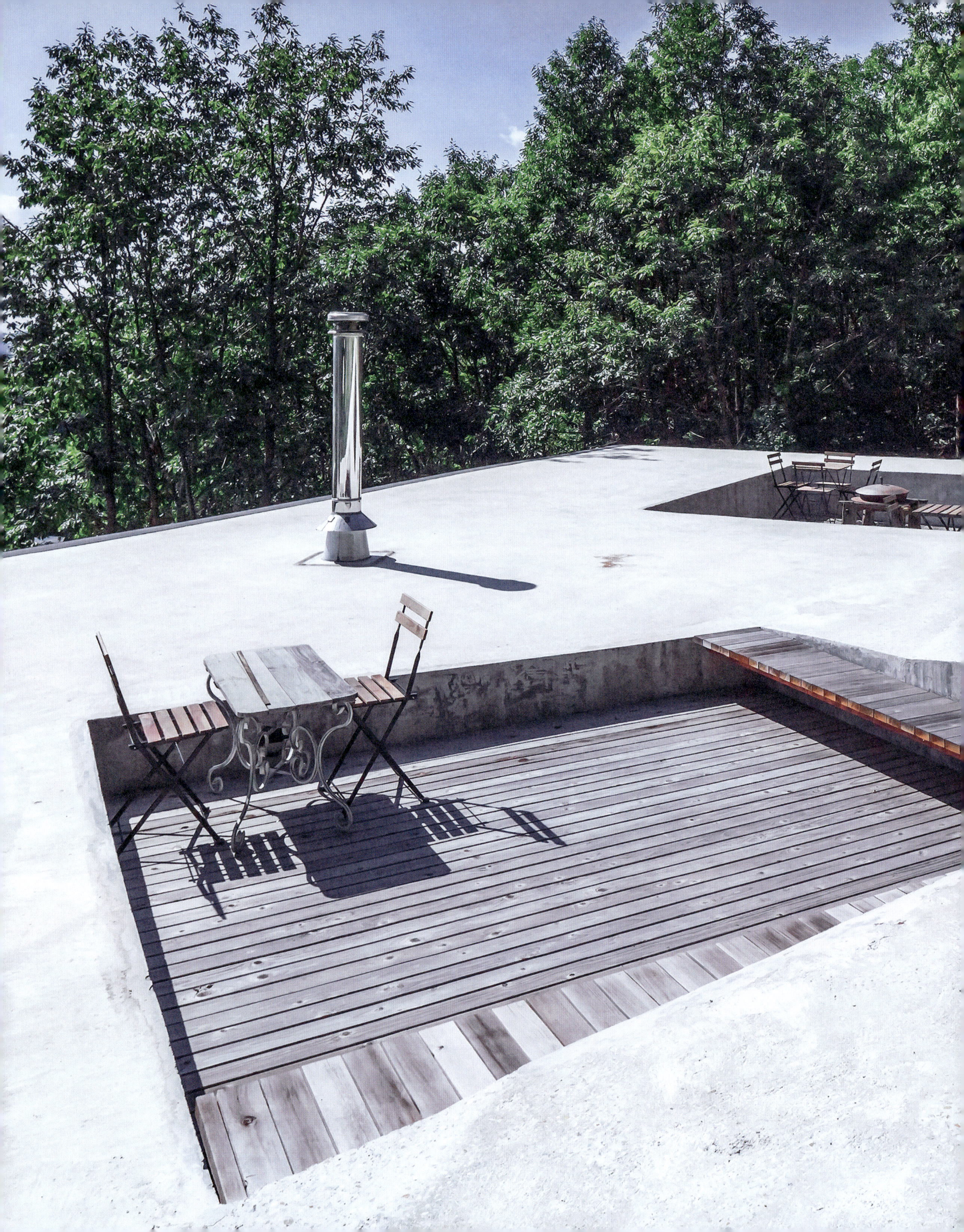

MK2

FURNITURE

2018

GALLERY

FLOOR PLAN:
SECOND-FLOOR APARTMENT

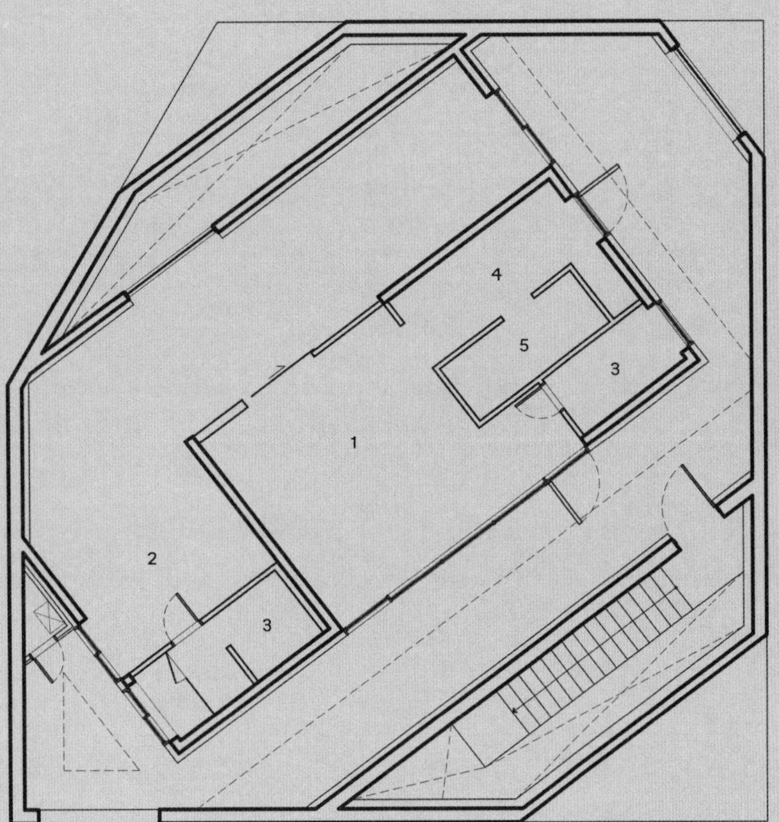

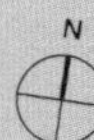

0 5m

1. Living room
2. Bedroom
3. Bathroom
4. Kitchen
5. Utility room
6. Furniture exhibition space

SECTION

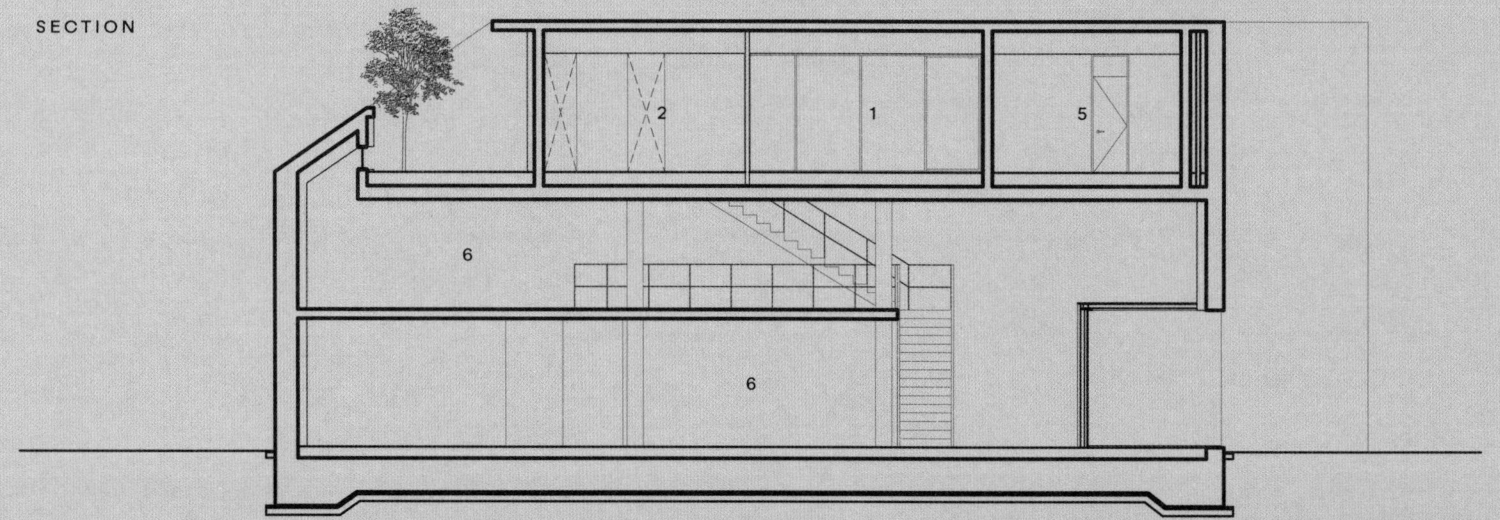

A couple – a furniture designer and a vintage furniture dealer (MK2) – longtime friends of mine, needed a house that could also function as a showroom. The site they had chosen lay in a rapidly developing suburban area east of Seoul, near the Bukhan River. The building was intended to accommodate furniture exhibitions for visiting guests while also serving as their private residence.

Surrounded by a patchwork of random buildings, the three-storey structure presents a minimalist, monolithic exterior. At street level, it aligns with its surroundings, broken only by large, wall-cut windows that frame selective views to the outside.

The ground and first floors, connected with an open stair, are conceived as uninterrupted spaces. The interior here is shaped by varying light conditions and ceiling heights. The slabs of the first and second floors are deliberately misaligned with the axis of the box-shaped plan, creating voids at the building's corners. This enables natural light to pour through these openings and spread throughout, enhancing the atmosphere of the exhibition space.

As one ascends, the building gradually transforms into a place of quiet retreat within the urban landscape. On the top floor, the owners' private residence is designed with skyward slits and openings, allowing ample daylight and ventilation as well as semi-private views of the surrounding neighbourhood.

LOCATION
Munho-gil, Seojong-myeon, Yangpyeong-gun, Gyeonggi-do, South Korea

GROSS FLOOR AREA
474.53 m^2 (5,108 sq. ft)

STRUCTURE
Reinforced concrete, exposed concrete finish

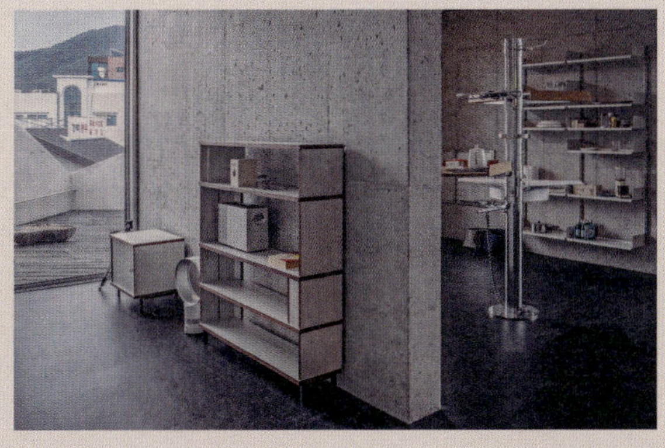

THIS PAGE
(above left) Windows break the monolithic exterior, framing selective views; (left) The entrance, leading directly into the exhibition space.

OPPOSITE
The first two floors are connected by an imposing concrete staircase.

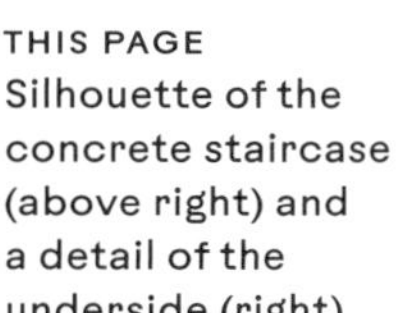

THIS PAGE
Silhouette of the concrete staircase (above right) and a detail of the underside (right).

OPPOSITE
The ground floor was conceived as an uninterrupted exhibition space.

ABOVE AND OPPOSITE
The owners' top-floor apartment blends neutral tones with exposed concrete and splashes of colour.

PP. 204–7
The apartment benefits from a wraparound rooftop terrace.

J I P Y O U N G G U E S T H O U S E

2 0 8 1

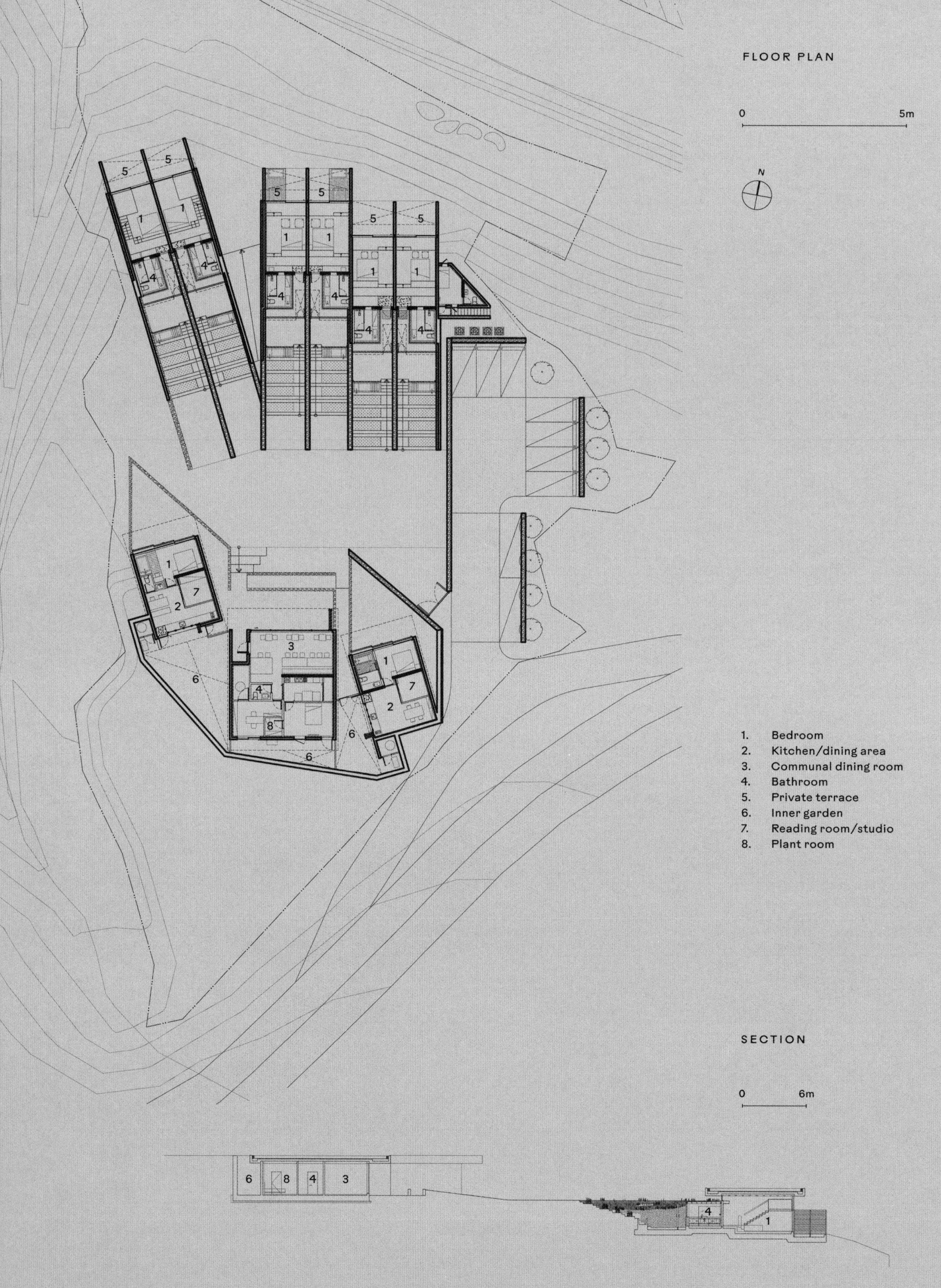
FLOOR PLAN
0
5m
N
1. Bedroom
2. Kitchen/dining area
3. Communal dining room
4. Bathroom
5. Private terrace
6. Inner garden
7. Reading room/studio
8. Plant room
SECTION
0
6m

Do we feel the fragility of human life when we see the mountains or the sea? If we get close to the earth, if we submerge ourselves in it, do we sense an essence closer to absolute being?

Jipyoung Guesthouse, perched on a cliff along the southern coast of South Korea, extroverts the experience of a home. Composed of eight guest units and a small communal dining area, the project is run by a local family and offers visitors a modest stay.

'Jipyoung' means 'horizon earth' in Korean. In fact, the building does not challenge the endless teal sea or crisp coastal air but instead humbly yields to the forces of nature around it, embedding the masses of the units in the landscape.

Whereas the predominant approach to seaside development in Korea has ravaged the natural coastline, Jipyoung Guesthouse seeks a healing embrace where it meets the earth. The overall site is below ground level, and the accommodation blocks are cut into the cliff in such a way that guests wake to an immersive view of the sea, experiencing the vitality of nature all around.

Built on challenging topography and bordered by a winding road, the blocks nestle within the natural folds of the hillside. My intention was to create an explicit communion between nature and architecture, a process through which those who occupy the guesthouses almost 'sink' into the landscape, immersing themselves in architecture that melts into the earth.

Along the outer walls that separate the units, deep grooves have been created where the concrete has been intentionally eroded. Using high-pressure water jets, local artisans sliced through the smooth surface of the concrete to expose its rough aggregate interior, which, in response to coastal conditions, allows a subtle layer of plant life to grow naturally. These sunken walls become a verdant expression of a relationship with nature based on humility and respect.

Jipyoung Guesthouse enacts a simple intervention into an existing landscape that strives at once to be embedded in the terrain and to become a truly special place of communion with nature. In the spaces between architecture and the earth, we connect with Mother Earth.

LOCATION
Changho-ri,
Sadeung-myeon,
Geoje-si,
Gyeongsangnam-do,
South Korea

GROSS FLOOR AREA
454.57 m^2 (4,893 sq. ft)

STRUCTURE
Reinforced concrete,
exposed concrete finish

THIS PAGE
Three blocks (above left) lie adjacent to the road. While two of these provide accommodation, the third (left) is used as a communal dining space, opening to a low-walled terrace and views of the sea.

OPPOSITE
Sections of angular concrete walls create semi-private outdoor spaces for guests.

BELOW AND OVERLEAF
The six units to the north offer studio-style accommodation. Each is accessed via wooden steps that lead down to a passage and a slatted gate.

OPPOSITE
Interior views of the accommodation blocks.

BELOW
Six of the units feature an external deck from which guests can enjoy uninterrupted views of the sea.

OPPOSITE
The walls between the units have been deliberately eroded with water jets to enable plant life to grow.

J I C H U K - D O N G H O U S E

2 0 2 2

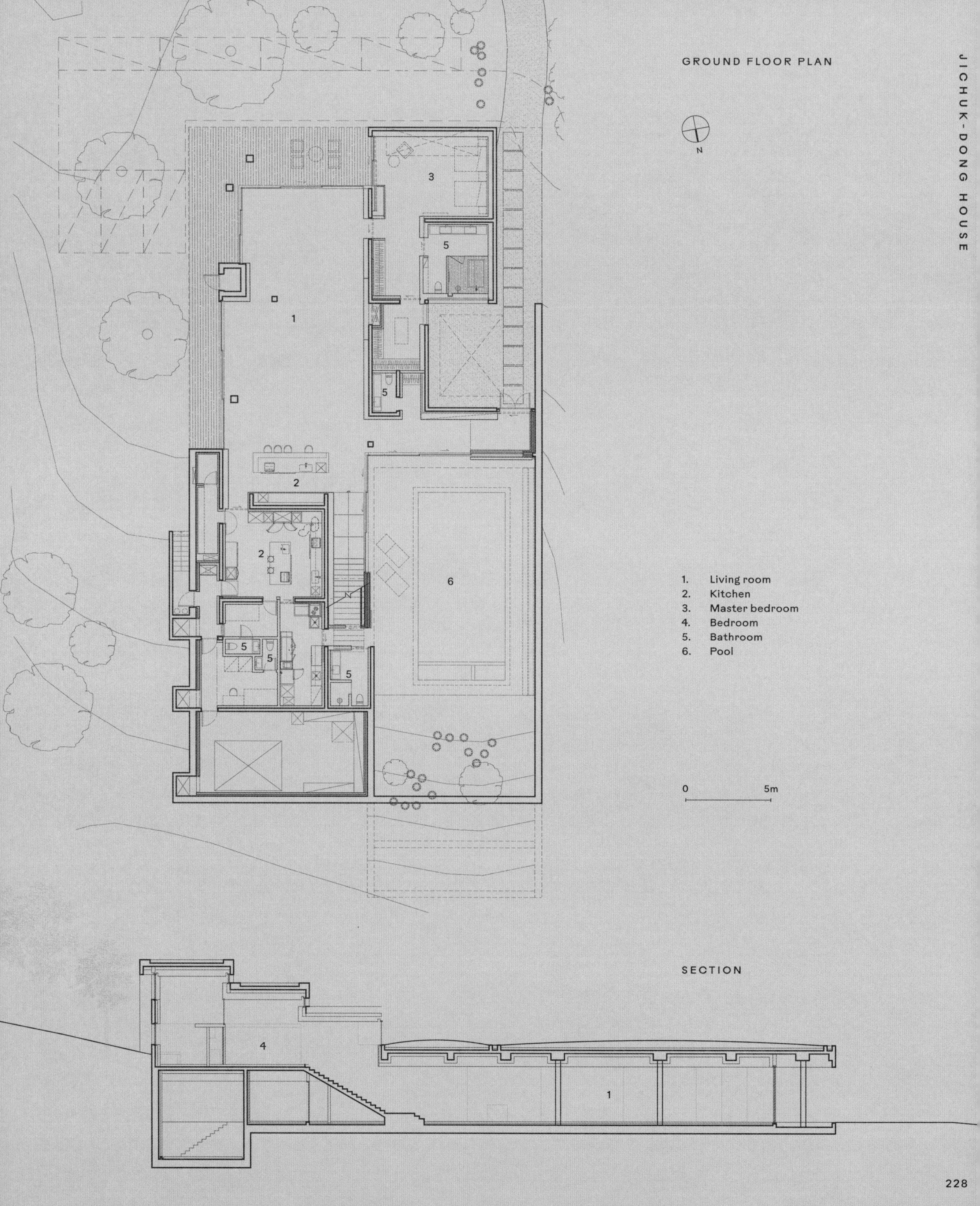
GROUND FLOOR PLAN
N
1
2
2
3
5
5
5
5
5
6
1. Living room
2. Kitchen
3. Master bedroom
4. Bedroom
5. Bathroom
6. Pool
0
5m
SECTION
4
1

Located on the outskirts of Goyang city, this weekend house offers a peaceful retreat for a three-generation family. Positioned at the base of a mountain, the house was conceived as a continuation of the landscape, integrating its form with the natural flow of the terrain. The volumes are carefully arranged to maintain visual openness and invite the elements in – air, light, water and earth.

Facing the hillside, the swimming pool creates a direct dialogue with the mountain, while the stepped massing of the first floor opens along the mountain's axis, allowing natural light and breezes to filter through the interior.

The house is organized across two floors to preserve a sense of privacy. The grandparents' master suite is located on the ground floor, while the children and their families occupy the first floor. Each level responds to the site in its own way: a quiet courtyard anchors the ground floor, while a rooftop garden offers expansive views and a more elevated connection to the outdoors. Throughout, the design seeks to immerse its inhabitants in nature, so that each moment spent in the house deepens their relationship with the surrounding landscape.

The house also benefits from an annexe where guests can stay. The annexe consists of a *hanok* and a dining pavilion, which is a modern extension. The story of this *hanok* is particularly interesting. It was built about twenty years ago on a beautiful site overlooking a river, where the owners used to live. The building is a faithful reconstruction of a 200-year-old traditional Korean house. During the construction of the current property, the *hanok* was dismantled and relocated to its present site, where it sits on a stone base. Relocating a *hanok* is not uncommon. In traditional Korean architecture, no nails are used; instead, wooden joints hold the structure together. This technique allows the buildings to be easily dismantled, moved and reassembled.

LOCATION
Jichuk-dong,
Deogyang-gu,
Goyang-si,
Gyeonggi-do,
South Korea

GROSS FLOOR AREA
648.26 m² (6,978 sq. ft)

STRUCTURE
Reinforced concrete,
exposed concrete finish

Porch (below) and a view of the house from the front (opposite).

Entrance (below)
and inner courtyard
(opposite).

BELOW AND OPPOSITE
Views of the annexe, which is composed of a *hanok* and a modern extension. Inside, there is a kitchen and dining area, as well as a bathroom equipped with a *hinoki* wood bathtub. These spaces are connected to the *hanok* rooms, creating areas where guests can stay.

BELOW AND OPPOSITE
A staircase leads down to a decked pool area. Large in-built cabinets provide plenty of storage.

PP. 242–43
The living room is flooded with light, with large sliding doors and clerestory windows on one side.

S L O P E D R O O F H O U S E

2 0 2 4

FLOOR PLAN
N
1. Swimming area
2. Barbecue area
3. Firepit
4. Living room and kitchen
5. Master bedroom
6. Bedroom
7. Bathroom
0
5m
SECTION

LOCATION
Sagye-ri, Andeok-myeon,
Seogwipo-si, Jeju-do,
South Korea

GROSS FLOOR AREA
220.64 m^2 (2,375 sq. ft)

STRUCTURE
Reinforced concrete,
exposed concrete,
aluminium perforated
panel

Jeju is geopolitically and scientifically significant, with the entire island designated as a UNESCO Global Geopark. Sometimes called the 'Hawaii of the East' because of its mild subtropical climate and unique culture, it is known for Hallasan, a dormant volcano and Korea's tallest peak, at 1,947 m (6,388 ft). Among its many other volcanic formations is Sanbangsan (395 m or 1,296 ft), a rare dome-shaped volcano on the southern coast that serves as a prominent landmark for miles around. I went to the site and thought that somehow the house has to emphasize these natural traits of Jeju.

A couple with four young children had recently moved to Jeju and wanted a second home nearby that could also accommodate guests. Sloped Roof House stands on a characterful site where the landscape descends gradually from Sanbangsan to the southern sea, following the path of ancient lava. I wanted the house to become a part of the flow of the mountain. The huge sloping roof continues, embraces and extends the land's rhythm, and creates spaces of varying heights and angles, offering dynamic spatial experiences both inside and out. The roof has two square openings that provide sheltered outdoor areas with views of the mountain and surrounding countryside. Below one of these openings, a swimming pool and deck have been incorporated; a firepit and barbecue define additional spaces for entertaining. These open areas, framed by the roof, emphasize the interplay between shelter, shadow and nature. The main interior space can be seen from the outside areas. Living room and kitchen are one open space, and the master bedroom and guest rooms are at opposite corners of the house. Every room faces outdoors.

The sloping roof is also designed to withstand the extreme weather on the island, which is known for strong winds and torrential downpours, especially during the summer typhoon period. In contrast to the traditional use of stone on the island, the design of Sloped Roof House mimics a dugout shelter, 'lifting' the land to create a place of refuge in the elevated earth. The interior spaces frame Sanbangsan, which stands as an enduring presence while the children play, laugh and make memories.

BELOW
A sheltered outdoor seating area has been created under the sweeping roof.

OVERLEAF
Night-time views of one of the bedrooms (left) and a social space (right).

THIS PAGE
One bedroom sits at a lower level than the rest of the house, offering a unique spatial experience.

OPPOSITE
Sequence of spaces from the guest quarters, through the living and dining area, towards the master bedroom at the far end.

P. 258
View from the master bedroom into the living area. The partitions over the door are transparent, allowing light to flood the space.

P. 259
Decked area and swimming pool.

PP. 260–61
Outdoor areas carved out of the sloping roof.

G I N K G O

2 0 2 4

T R E E

H O U S E

PRINCIPAL ELEVATION: THE TWO RENOVATED STRUCTURES, WITH THE NEWLY CONSTRUCTED GINKGO TREE HOUSE ON THE RIGHT

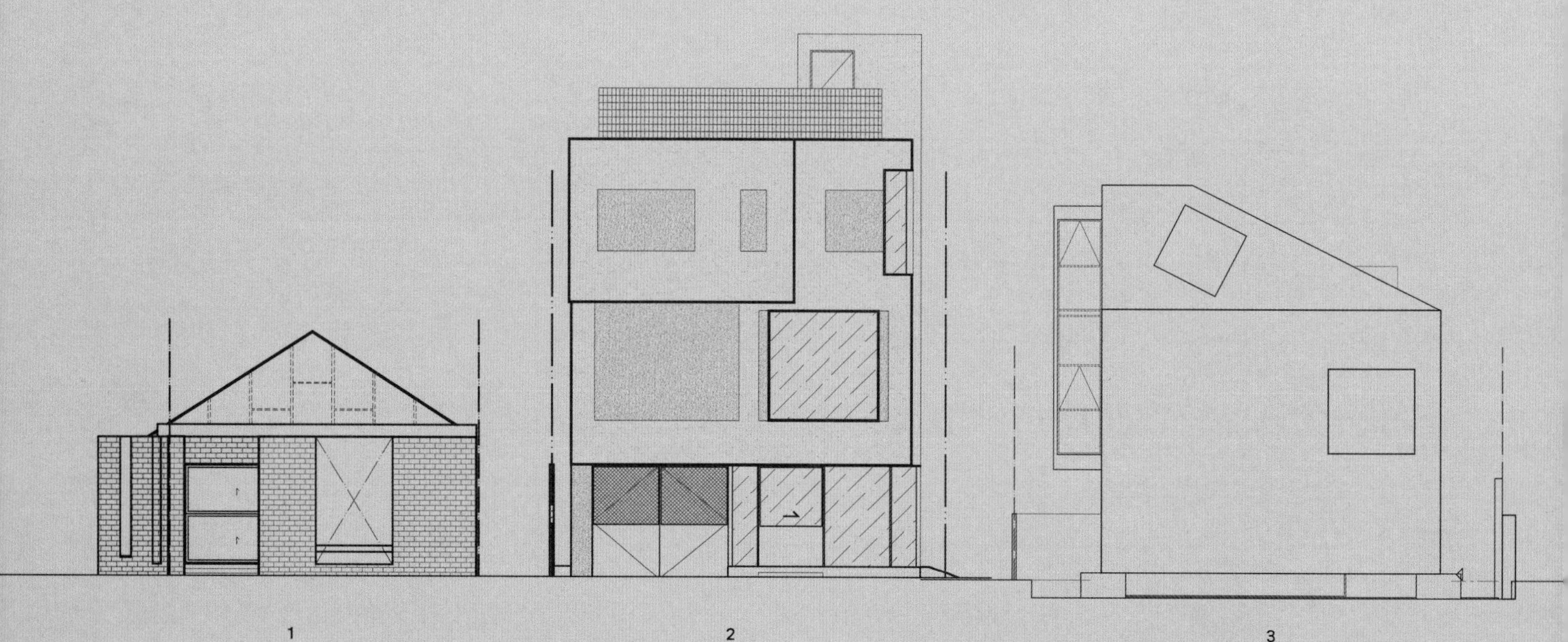

1. Existing building, renovated
2. Existing building, renovated
3. New building (exhibition space, with accommodation on the top floor)

GROUND FLOOR PLAN

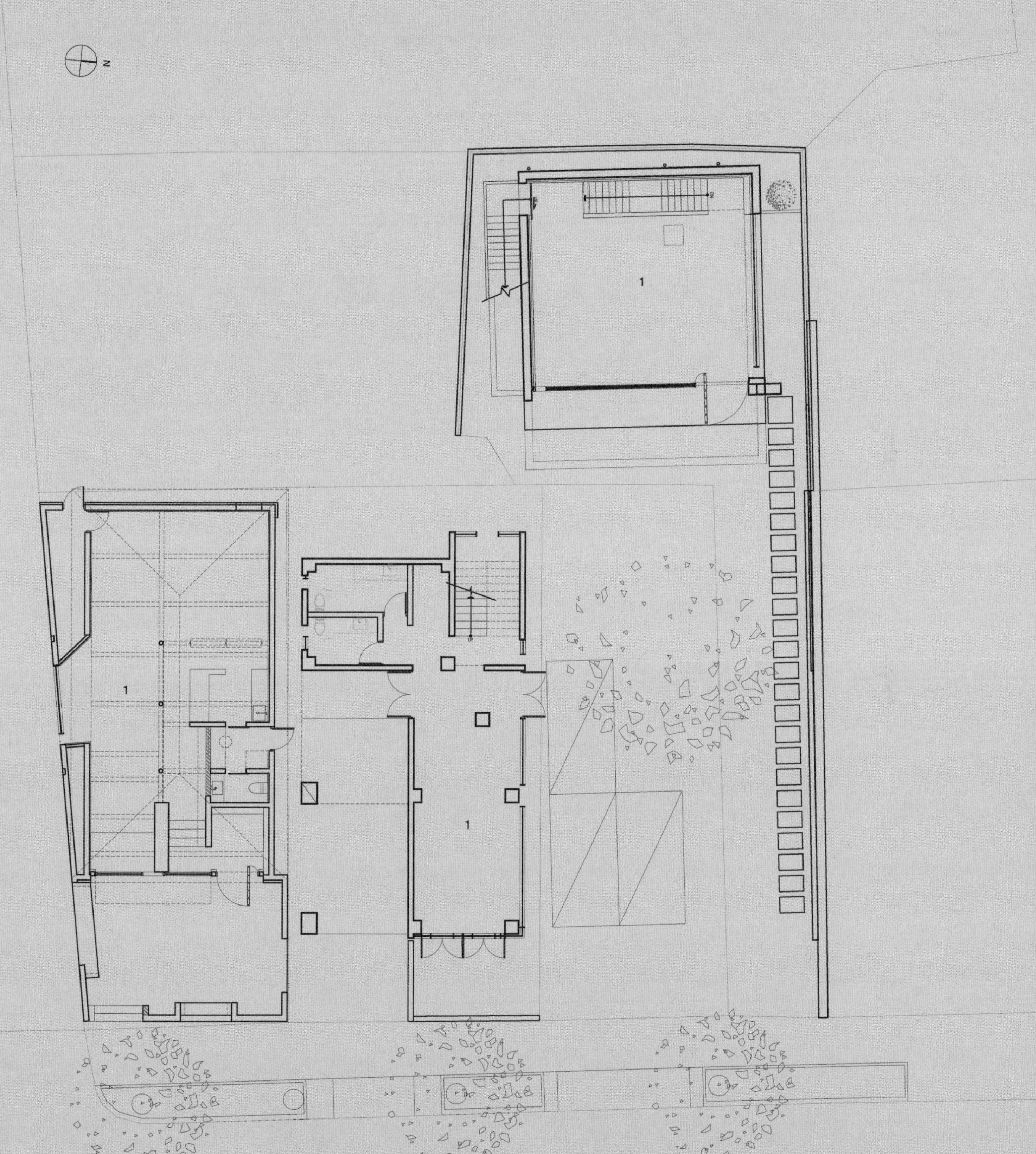

1. Exhibition space

Ginkgo Tree House is a newly constructed building in a largely residential area of Seoul. It was commissioned by Youk Shim-won, an artist known for her colourful portraits that celebrate women, and her husband, who manages two existing gallery spaces adjacent to the site, which we also renovated as part of this project. Youthquake Gallery is the name of the complex as a whole, covering all three spaces.

Renovations to the two existing spaces were extensive. In one of the buildings, the Gallery Jin building, which dates from the late 1970s, we tore down a heavy cement wall that faced the street to reveal the *hanok* behind and open up the structure to the street. Above the newly exposed courtyard, we installed gabion panels topped with artificially shaped stones. These elements were used to contrast the openness of the *hanok* with a sense of boundary and weight, reinforcing a subtle tension between enclosure and exposure.

For the new building, the clients asked us to come up with a design that centres around a beautiful ginkgo tree, which they considered the site's main feature. Our approach was to create a building that serves as a harmonious backdrop, preserving the tree's prominence. The ground floor, which functions as the entrance hall, is used as an exhibition space. It was necessary to block the view from the outside to enhance the viewing experience inside. The façade is raised around 60 cm (23½ in.) from the ground, so that the wall appears to float. A small garden at the front slopes down towards the building and extends under the floating wall into the ground-floor area, giving the impression that the landscape flows into the structure itself.

The first and second floors have a variety of uses, with spaces functioning as private offices and accommodation, as well as tea rooms for greeting guests. The first floor encourages visitors to appreciate the ginkgo tree through a square window facing the garden, while on the second floor a diamond-shaped window drilled into the sloping roof provides a dramatic view of the tree's fronds and the sky. The circulation culminates in a terrace on the second floor, where a spacious outdoor area offers a final glimpse of the tree and a view of Gyeongbokgung Palace in the background.

LOCATION
Tongui-dong, Jongno-gu, Seoul, South Korea

GROSS FLOOR AREA
332.15 m² (3,575 sq. ft)

STRUCTURE
Reinforced concrete, exposed concrete, brick

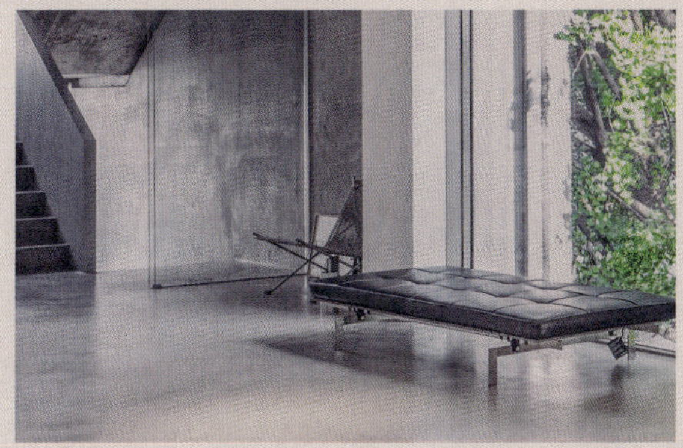

자하문로6길
Jahamun-ro 6-gil
34→1
HYOJA-RO 25, JONGNO-GU
FRITZ HANSEN
27

BELOW
The complex from the street, with the ginkgo tree on the right.

OVERLEAF, LEFT
Entrance to the exhibition space in the Gallery Jin building, an existing structure that was extensively renovated. Gyeongbokgung Palace can be glimpsed through the opening in the wall.

OVERLEAF, RIGHT
Inside the Gallery Jin building, which occupies a former *hanok*. Light filters through gaps in the original wooden roof, casting unique shadows in the exhibition space.

Poul Kjærholm
31ST MAY - 7TH JULY 2024
HYOJA-RO 25, JONGNO-GU, SEOUL, KOREA
FRITZ HANSEN
Poul Kjærholm
27

ABOVE
First-floor view towards Gyeongbokgung Palace from the newly constructed Ginkgo Tree House.

OPPOSITE
Façade of the central building in the complex, which was also renovated and functions as an exhibition space.

BELOW
The ginkgo tree remains a prominent feature of the site, with the buildings providing a harmonious backdrop.

OPPOSITE
The front of the newly constructed Ginkgo Tree House.

P. 278
The façade of the new building floats above the ground, blurring the boundaries between exterior and interior.

P. 279
A dramatic opening on the top floor offers views of the ginkgo tree.

S O U T H

C A P E

P R O J

E C T

The South Cape Owners Club is a luxury resort located on Changseon Island, off the southern tip of the Korean Peninsula. Set along an unspoiled stretch of coastline, the site lies within an area of exceptional natural beauty.

This landscape is familiar to me – around 2010, I was invited to design the masterplan, the Linear Suite and some residences here. For this new project, the task was to design twenty-three individual residences across the east wing of the site – hidden and dramatic – offering resort guests a deeply immersive experience within this singular environment. I approached the masterplan as a land art installation. The masses of the residential units were conceived not as isolated objects, but as elements in a wider composition – meant to be experienced sequentially and spatially, as one moves through the site.

The concept of land architecture undoubtedly carries a debt to the environmental art experimentation of the 1960s and '70s in the United States – works by Richard Serra, Robert Smithson, or Alberto Burri's Grande Cretto in Sicily, for instance.

While these approaches may seem aligned at a broader level, their orientation and aims differ significantly. My concern was not the sculptural aspect of each house itself, but the desire to inhabit the landscape while preserving its identity and integrity. This approach is grounded in what Christian Norberg-Schulz in his studies described as the spirit of the place, or *genius loci*. To protect this sense of place, architecture must ultimately become part of the landscape – just as buildings have traditionally done in the Korean context.

The key consideration was how to intervene in the landscape without damaging the existing terrain and the natural environment. This concern can be broadly broken down into three main elements: topography, ecology, and the interplay of light and wind. Rather than functioning independently, these elements are closely linked to the land and the ocean, influencing the form, scale and orientation of the structure, as well as the materials used to build it. The result is three distinct types of residence that actively reflect the terrain, the views and the natural conditions. Each of the twenty-three units functions independently and includes two bedrooms, two bathrooms, a living area, a kitchen and a private outdoor space (*madang*).

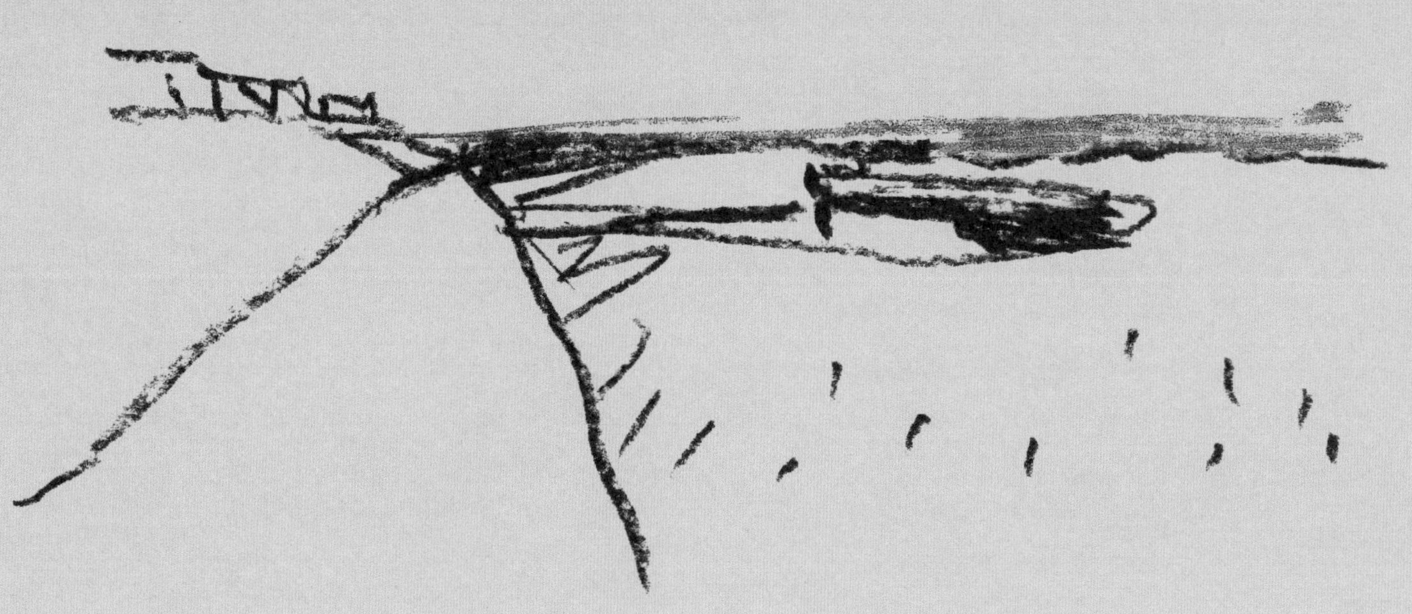

Type A (11 units) is positioned on the upper hillside. Here, the architecture follows the contours of the slope, allowing the structures to nestle into the terrain. Rather than being placed on top of the landscape, the buildings are embedded within it – blending into the earth and preserving the continuous, flowing topography. The design emphasizes the transition between interior and exterior, responding to the land's natural undulations to generate a coherent spatial experience. Inside, at the heart of the living area, a sunken gathering zone – 70 cm (27½ in.) below floor level – offers a stripped-back yet intimate setting where guests can sit, converse and engage with the space in a tactile, grounded way.

The other two residential types, positioned on the lower side of the hill, engage with the site's road-facing views – an essential characteristic of this area and a key element I considered when shaping the land-art masterplan.

Type B (7 units), located at the entrance to the site, is not immediately visible. The building merges with the terrain's downward slope towards the sea, dissolving into the land's natural contours. This approach recalls the design logic of the Jipyoung Guesthouse, where similar attention was given to minimizing visual impact and preserving continuity with the landscape.

Despite its proximity to the entrance, Type B maintains a discreet presence. Its form follows the natural topography and integrates with existing vegetation, ensuring open views across the site remain unobstructed. Accessing the unit requires descending slightly, an intentional shift in elevation that allows the ocean view to emerge, framed by a floating roof plane. As one approaches the interior, the landscape seems to flow through the architecture – from the hilltop, across the living space, and finally out towards the horizon, where it dissolves into the ocean.

In contrast, **Type C** residences (5 units) are designed to reveal themselves gradually – as one approaches, enters and moves through the site. Their placement and form encourage a slow unfolding of the architecture, heightening spatial and perceptual awareness. Long horizontal glass openings draw light deep into the interiors while immersing the viewer in the surrounding landscape. Reflections, projections and subtle colour shifts on the glazed surfaces generate a visual rhythm that transforms the experience into a form of land art.

To intensify this effect, the units are orientated at carefully calculated angles, each establishing a distinct dialogue with the terrain. This variation in orientation deepens the interplay between built form and natural context.

LOCATION
Jindong-ri,
Changseon-myeon,
Namhae-gun,
Gyeongsangnam-do,
South Korea

TYPE A

1. Living/dining area
2. Master bedroom
3. Bathroom
4. Guest room
5. Terrace
6. External bath
7. Garden

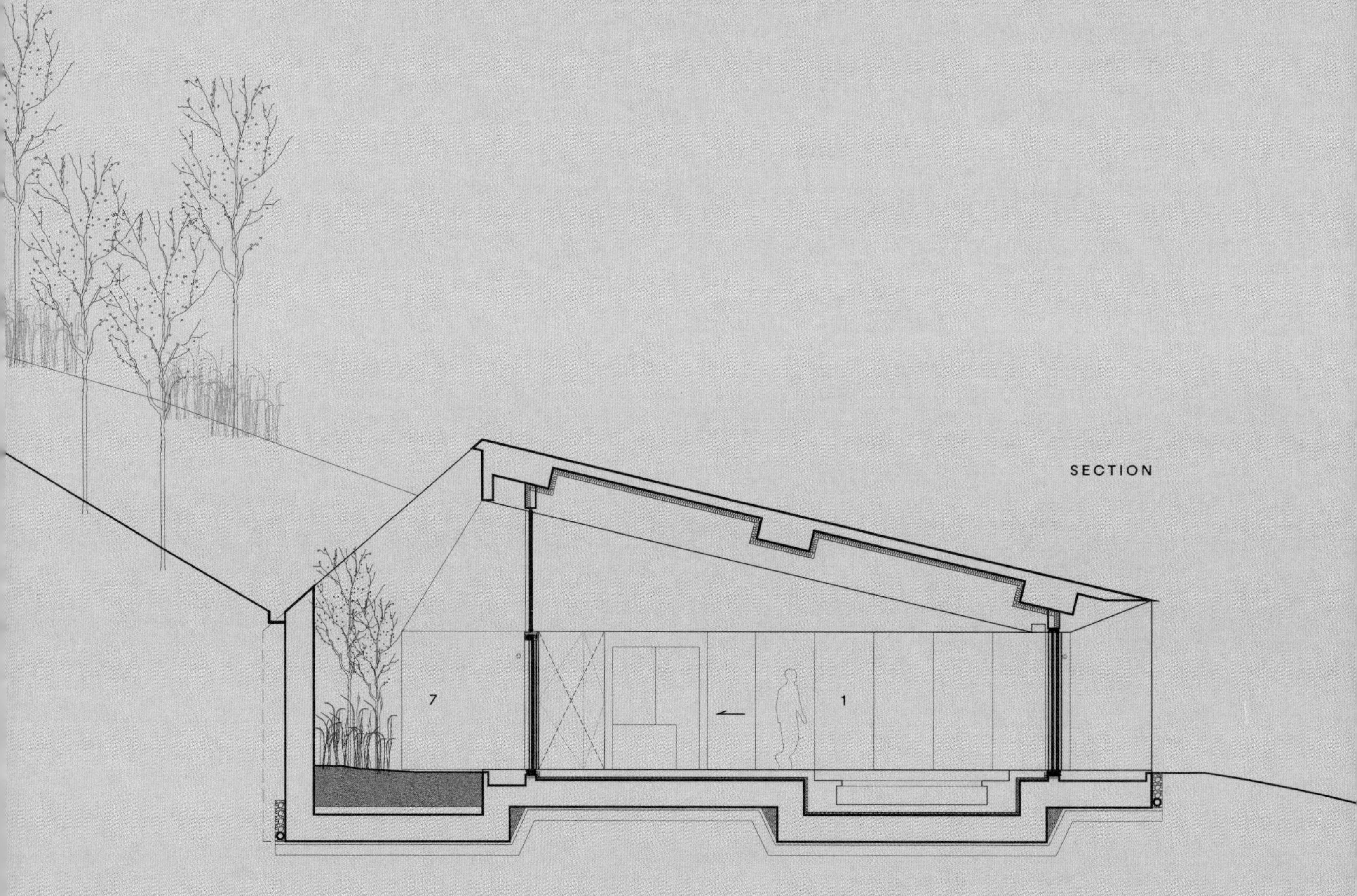

FLOOR PLAN

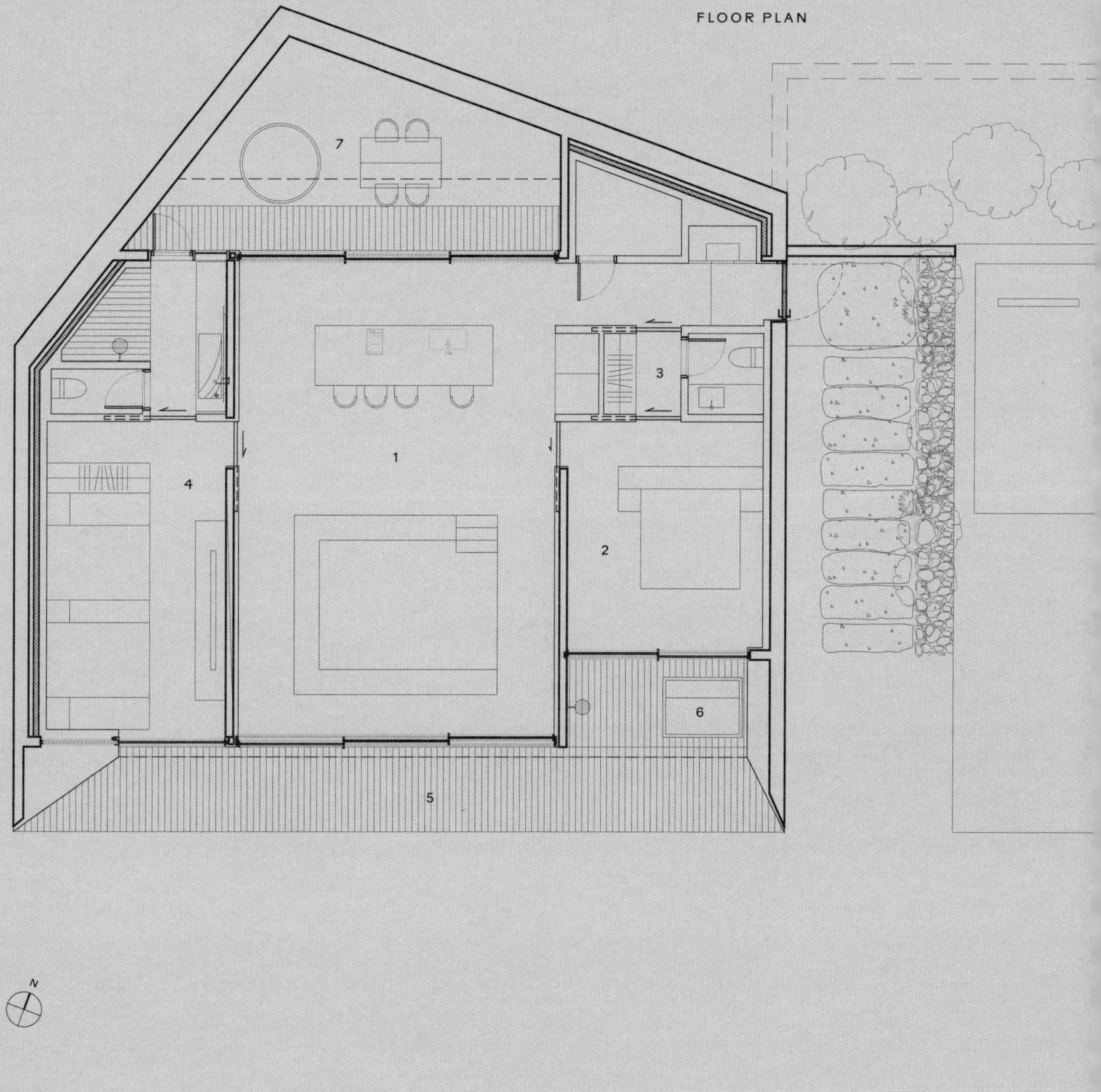

7

3

1

4

2

6

5

0 5m

Type A units, on the upper hillside, are embedded in the landscape, responding to the contours of the terrain. Renderings: from the road (this page); and looking into the interior (opposite), with the central living area and a bedroom on either side.

LEFT AND OVERLEAF
View of the living/dining area. Openings on opposite sides create a continuous flow through the space, from uphill to downhill, following the natural slope of the land.

TYPE B

1. Living/dining area
2. Master bedroom with en-suite
3. Guest room
4. Bathroom
5. Pool

SECTION

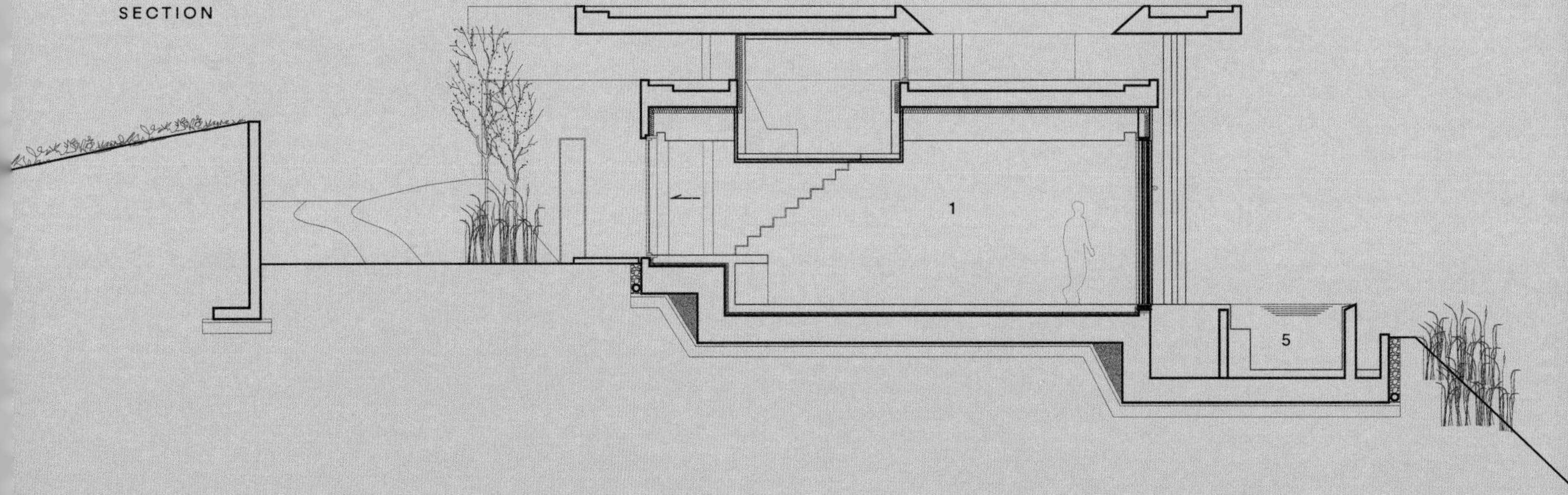

0 5m

FLOOR PLAN

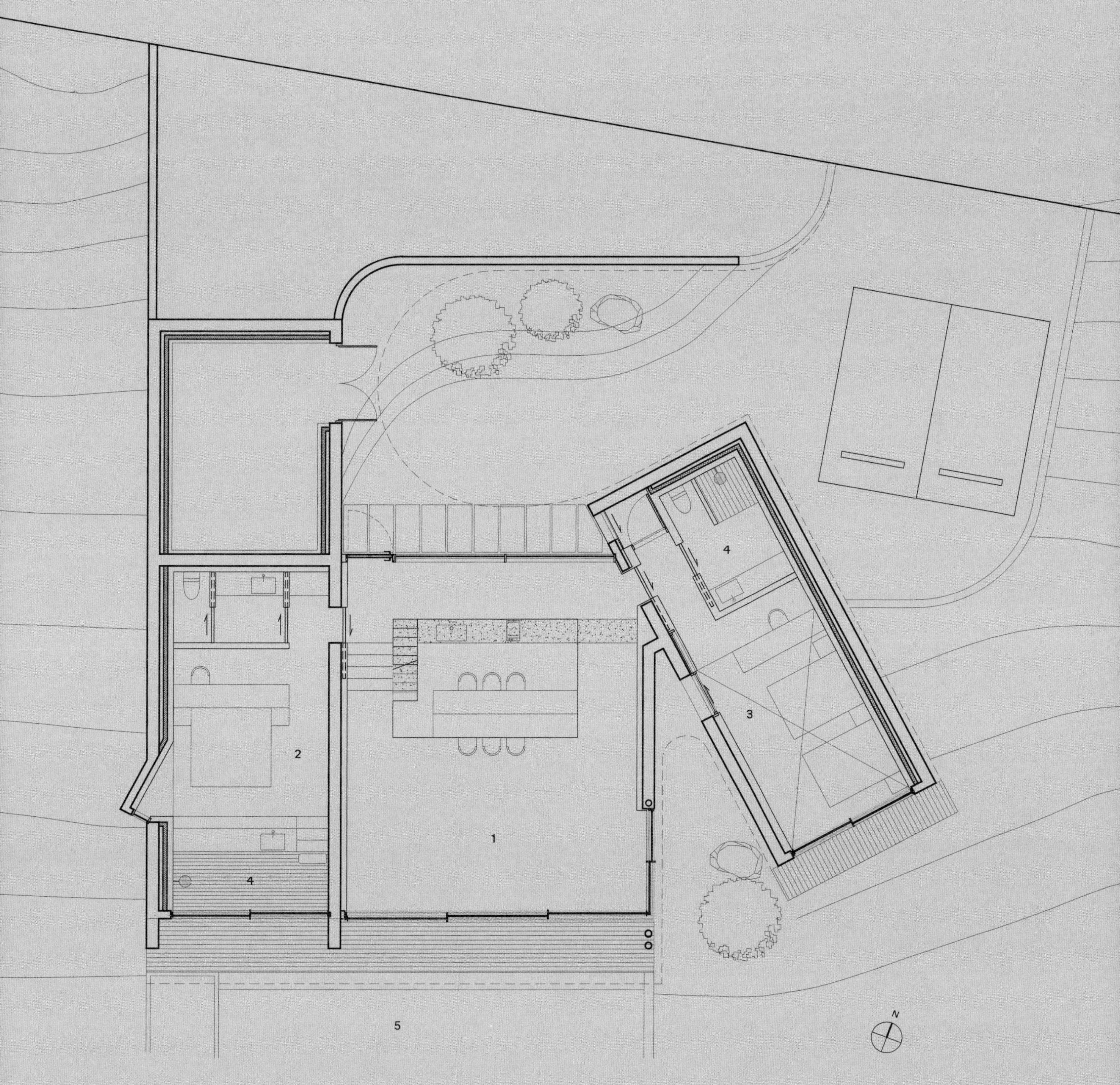

Type B units, at the entrance to the site, are designed to sink into the land. Renderings: view from the road (below and opposite, above) and looking into the living area (opposite, below).

The entrance leads directly into the kitchen and open-plan living area (opposite, below). Renderings of the guest room (above) and master bedroom (opposite, above).

TYPE C

1. Living room
2. Bedroom
3. Bathroom
4. Pool
5. Plant room

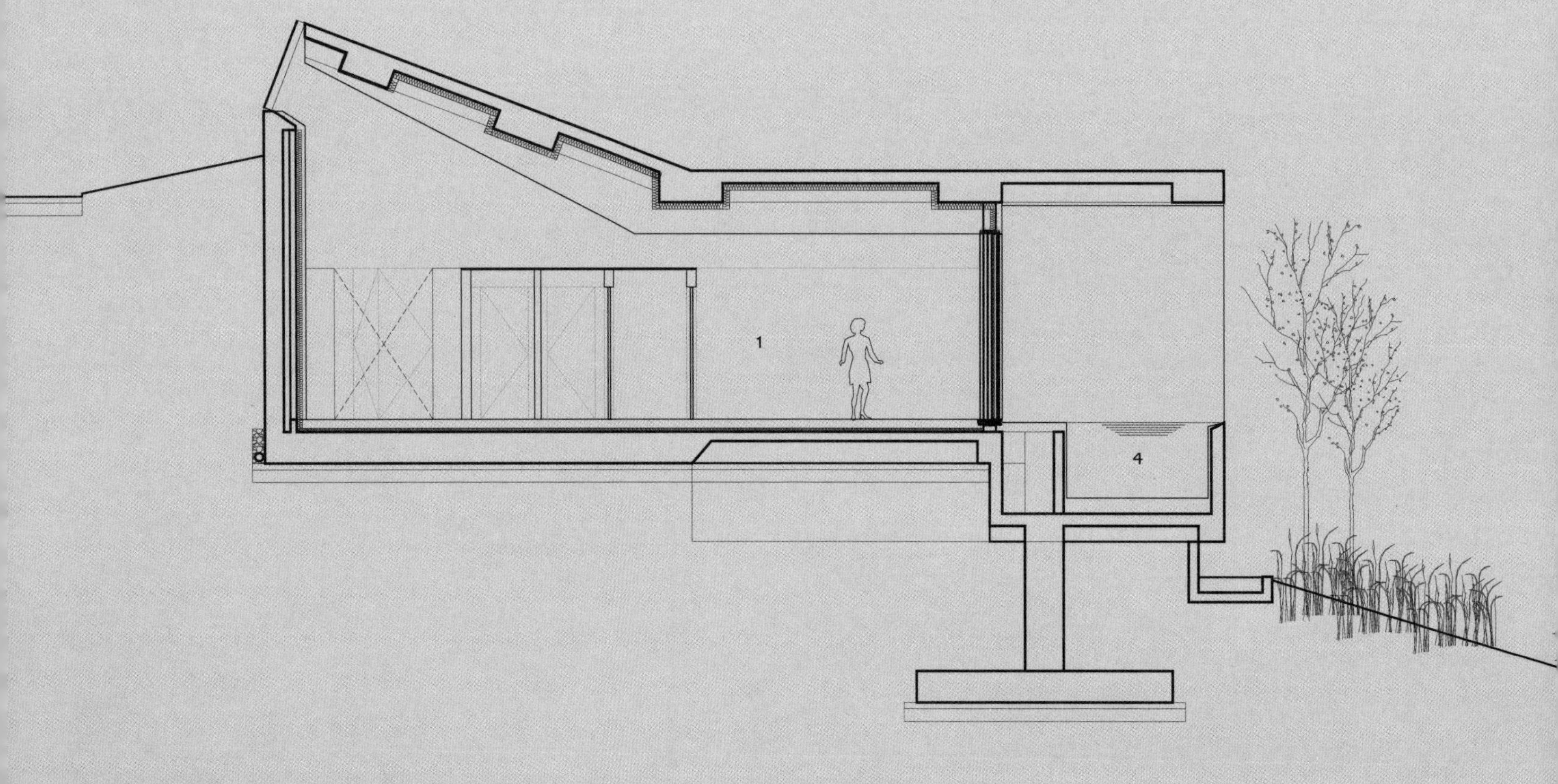

SECTION

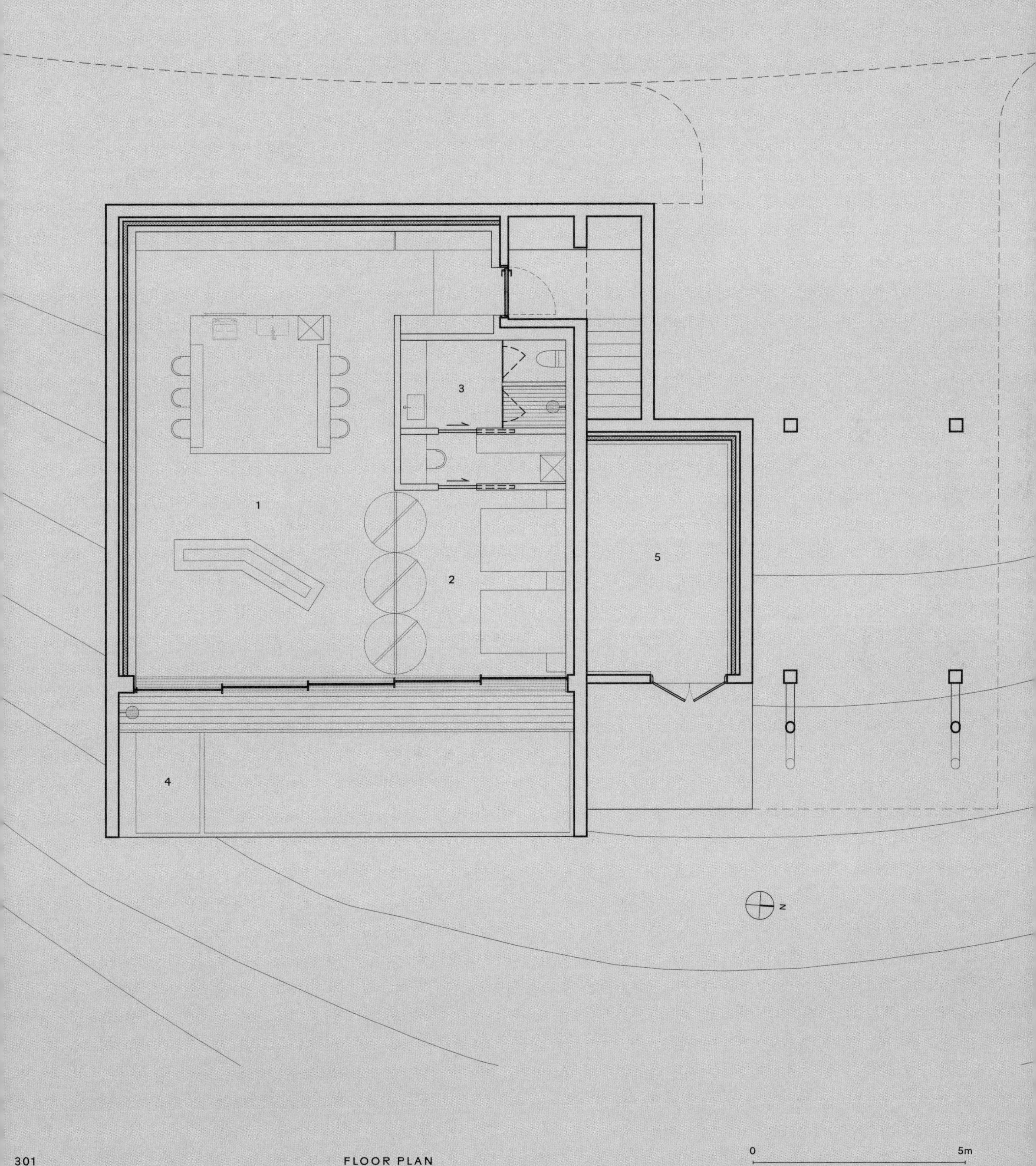

FLOOR PLAN

Type C units are designed to reveal themselves gradually. Renderings of the exterior (above and right) and the living area/bedroom (pp. 304–5).

Byoung Cho's architecture begins with restrained form and draws close to the earth. It becomes part of the land – sometimes continuing its flow, sometimes supplementing it with physical form. When architecture gently seeps into the earth, its visible shape recedes into the background, allowing us to focus more acutely on the space itself. Through such essential spatial experiences, Cho puts an emphasis on the user's bodily perception and emotional resonance. His long-standing architectural concern has been the coexistence of nature and built form – how buildings respond to the land, to the flow of water, light and wind.

Cho's unwavering architectural values – prioritizing the experience of space over form, taking an assimilative approach to the land, and composing relationships between exterior and interior – are rooted in the *hanok* of his childhood, in his pursuit of an architecture infused with emotion, and in his belief in rational, hands-on building. These ideas extend outwards into notions such as contemporary vernacular, Cho's 'design-build' method (a way of working in which design and construction are considered simultaneously), and an aesthetic sensibility he describes as *mak* or *mahk* (meaning 'imperfection').

Cho spent his early years in a compact *hanok* in downtown Seoul. At just 20 *pyeong* (about 66 m² or 710 sq. ft), this was a *dosi hanok* – urban traditional housing, developed in the 1930s and '40s to accommodate increasing city density. L- or U-shaped in plan, these houses were tightly built against neighbouring homes, yet retained central courtyards that opened to the sun and sky. Cho's childhood home, like others of its type, was densely packed into the urban fabric, but its south-facing orientation welcomed sunlight, and its courtyard channelled the breeze. The 3 × 3 m (10 × 10 ft) courtyard was at once his playground and his refuge, a place where he could fully experience the weather and atmosphere of each season.

Cho often says it's not the architectural 'space' he remembers, but the physical experiences of living in it. Cold air would filter through the *hanji*-paper windows in winter, but the floor stayed warm with *ondol* heating. He vividly recalls the flickering shadows of tree branches on the translucent screens at night, the silhouettes of family members glimpsed across the *daecheong* floor, the rain trickling down, the glare of sunlight, and the crisp blue sky framed by the courtyard. These are his most dramatic spatial memories. Equally formative were the natural environments of Sangju, his father's hometown, which he visited every school holiday, and which at the time had not yet been touched by urban development, its forests and fields offering him raw, primordial experiences of nature.

After finishing high school, Cho, who had always loved making things, studied ceramics for a short period, following a friend to Byeokje, an area that is well known for ceramic production in Goyang, Gyeonggi Province, on the northwestern edge of Seoul. However, it wasn't long before doubt set in. 'It was quiet and peaceful,' he recalls. 'I enjoyed touching and shaping clay, but I found the unpredictability of firing – how the flames could completely change the outcome – disappointing.' In 1981, an architecture exhibition opened at the newly completed Sejong Center for the Performing Arts in Gwanghwamun, Seoul. There, he encountered architectural drawings for the very first time. Something clicked. This was the moment he decided to pursue architecture.

Not long after, in January 1982, he set off for the United States, without a clear plan, but with the vague hope that he might study somewhere near the birthplace of Mark Twain (in Florida, Missouri). 'At a second-hand bookstore near Cheonggyecheon [Seoul], I came across Twain's *What Is Man?*' Cho says. 'I was shocked by how bleakly he portrayed humanity. It left me with a huge question: are humans truly driven only by self-interest? Isn't life something more beautiful and positive than that? Many years later, I came to understand that the book emphasized a worldview centred entirely on reason. But even so, I couldn't bring myself to dismiss emotion. That realization – that rationality alone was not enough – stayed with me.'

The encounter with Twain marked a turning point, the beginning of a lifelong philosophical inquiry, and a response that would shape both his architecture and his view of life itself: if reason was insufficient, then what else must architecture hold? That tension – between intellect and feeling – became the foundation for his pursuit of architecture infused with sensitivity and belief in humanity.

A vague interest in the American West eventually led him to the quiet setting of the University of Montana. Life at the university, set in a peaceful rural landscape, was uneventful and subdued. Yet one day, without intention, Cho happened to look up at the sky and was immediately struck by the quiet beauty hidden in the mundane surroundings of the countryside. Though the landscape seemed unremarkable at first, he was suddenly awakened to the presence of nature in its most subtle form.

Montana's agricultural barns made a particular impression on him. With their stripped-down forms and unembellished utility, these structures stirred something within him. He felt that these barns – built not for style but for purpose – shared a kinship with traditional Korean architecture. They were free from pretence. They were buildings born of necessity. Built from the simplest of materials with the most direct of methods, they had a kind of raw, essential quality that resonated deeply.

It was here that Cho's lifelong interest in practicality and spontaneous beauty began to take shape. What he saw in those barns wasn't a lack of refinement – it was a form of truthfulness. That honesty in construction, born of constraints, became one of his enduring architectural principles.

EXPERIENCE AND PERCEPTION

After graduating from the University of Montana and gaining several years of practical experience, in 1988 Cho entered the Harvard Graduate School of Design to pursue more in-depth research. There, he began to engage in earnest with his central theme: experience and perception in architecture. At the time, Western architectural discourse was entering a period of self-reflection and critique, particularly in response to the heroic narratives of modernism.

'Alberto Pérez-Gómez's book *Architecture and the Crisis of Modern Science* had a profound influence on me,' Cho explains. 'So did Kenneth Frampton's essay "Towards a Critical Regionalism". These texts didn't reject modern architecture outright, but they did call into question its excesses: its obsession with image, monumentality and visual spectacle. For Cho, this critique struck a chord. 'I came to believe that meaningful architecture isn't something monumental or photogenic – it's something that speaks to nature, and to humanity. And I thought that Korean architecture could offer a real alternative.'

This period of study, unfolding in the late 1980s, coincided with a broader architectural movement that challenged the tenets of International Style modernism. While others turned towards postmodern pastiche or deconstructivist form, Cho sought a less-travelled path rooted in the quiet, unassuming logic of traditional Korean building. In this, he aligned closely with the principles of critical regionalism: embracing the progressive ambitions of modern architecture while anchoring it in place, culture and structure.

Rather than rejecting modernism, Cho wanted to uncover what it had missed: abstraction that was warm rather than cold, logic that was responsive rather than imposed. He believed these qualities could be found in Eastern philosophy, particularly Daoism, and in the traditional Korean approach to building, which seeks to harmonize with nature instead of dominating it.

'I once read a paper by the art historian Ko Yu-seop, where he described Korean painting as "an experiential image into which the body enters". That struck me deeply. I realized I had always felt a kind of emptiness in visual beauty alone. I was beginning to feel that form, when created only for the sake of appearance, was no more than a shell.'

Cho found himself increasingly drawn to the characteristics of traditional Korean wooden architecture, especially its ability to merge gently with its natural surroundings. What appealed to him most was its sense of ease: architecture that neither exaggerated nor over-defined, but rather settled into the land with quiet confidence. This was not architecture that demanded attention – it invited calm. It was neither overly refined nor carelessly rustic, but simply comfortable. To Cho, this was not merely a visual impression, but a spatial experience that resided in the body, as well as the eyes. It was this realization that led him to the notion of experiential architecture – an architecture that reaches beyond visual proportions and geometric form, and instead engages the senses through direct spatial experience.

More than anything, Cho was drawn to the earth. He believed architecture should respond to the ground – not float above it, but descend into it, conform to it, and at times even become part of it. Like the *hanok*, which negotiates with the topography through a stone stylobate (*gidan*, or raised platform), and steps down into the land, Cho sought to create architecture that wasn't placed *on* the land, but *within* it – architecture that listens, yields and is absorbed into the land.

This philosophy began to take shape through several conceptual projects he undertook while at the Harvard Graduate School of Design – most notably the Lugano Project, developed in 1990 during an exchange at ETH Zurich, and the Boston Project, completed at Harvard in 1991. In both, he explored the sensation of entering into the earth, both literally and metaphorically. In the Lugano Project, he proposed building a large wall in front of Lake Lugano, in Switzerland, and designed an approach where one descends a narrow staircase along the wall before reaching the lake. The Boston Project sought to preserve the character of alleyways while creating an experiential spatial sequence. For his graduate thesis project, he designed a simple box and focused on the experiential process of entering the space – ultimately revealing his deep-seated fascination with the idea of entering into the earth. These were not mere design exercises – they were thought experiments, prototypes of perception.

This trajectory culminated in his graduation thesis at Harvard, in which Cho pursued the theme of experience and perception through a spatial experiment. The project proposed a simple square box buried underground. At its centre, it opened into a hollow square – shaped like the Korean letter 'ㅁ' (pronounced as 'm'). Visitors descended into the structure via a narrow staircase. As they moved downwards, the presence of architecture began to disappear. Light began to fall differently. A small courtyard, open to the sky, revealed itself. Form receded. Atmosphere emerged.

The entire project was an inquiry into the *origin* of architecture: how do we experience space as we enter it? How does that experience shape our perception of nature? And how do structure and void – the solid and the empty – form relationships that we can feel, even if we cannot always explain it?

Within the quiet geometry of this square box, Cho placed his own childhood memories: the shadows in narrow alleys, the faint light from lanterns, the scent of wet earth after rain. These were not metaphors – they were spatial memories carried in his body.

Just as traditional Korean architecture uses layout and orientation to achieve harmony with nature – rather than relying on overt visual display – Cho believed that emotional resonance could be created not by adding, but by removing. That spatial emotion – born from shadow, scale, wind and silence – was, to him, the most powerful architectural experience.

Moreover, to embed nature into architecture wasn't simply poetic – it was, in his mind, deeply sustainable. This belief naturally extended into a growing interest in renovation and reuse. 'It's not that I had a particular desire to do adaptive reuse,' he reflects. 'But I was drawn to the idea of not demolishing a building – to reinterpreting it. Before worrying about saving materials, I wanted to ask: what can we do with something that already exists as part of the land?'

A CONTEMPORARY VERNACULAR DISCOVERED IN THE *DALDONGNAE*

Upon returning to Korea, Cho found himself drawn to the informal hillside settlements of Seoul's Jeongneung-dong and Sindang-dong – neighbourhoods (*dong*) often referred to as *daldongnae*, or 'moon villages'. These settlements emerged during Korea's rapid industrialization in the 1960s and '70s, as the urban poor built makeshift homes on steep hillsides where land was cheap and development unregulated. Though lacking infrastructure and poorly connected by public transport, these dense clusters of self-built homes earned their poetic name from being high up, 'close to the moon'. Many of these structures have since been torn down and redeveloped, but Cho saw in the moon villages a raw, unfiltered Korean vernacular – one shaped not by architectural ambition, but by the necessities of the time, the terrain and the spirit of community.

While researching the urban fabric of Sindang-dong, Cho sought to learn the principles of traditional Korean architecture from Professor Shi-chun Jung. In a book that Cho wrote and illustrated based on his research, published in 1997, Jung contributed an essay titled 'The Korean Sense of Space', in which he outlined the characteristics of an ideal Korean residential site. Drawing on *pungsu* (a Korean version of the Chinese feng shui) – an East Asian geomantic tradition concerned with interpreting and utilizing land – he described how orientation and site placement are determined by natural forces such as mountains, water and wind. This nature-orientated approach to spatial organization is evident in UNESCO-listed villages such as Hahoe (Andong) and Yangdong (Gyeongju), where the hierarchy and boundaries of the community are aligned with natural flows of terrain, wind direction and the southern orientation of homes. Key principles include *baesanimsu* (背山臨水), a location backed by mountains and facing water. Jung also emphasized how organically formed paths often converge at intersections to create communal courtyards.

Cho noticed that the *daldongnae* neighbourhoods still followed these principles, albeit unconsciously. The winding paths and stepped courtyards, though now paved in concrete or brick instead of straw and clay, flowed naturally with the contours of the land. Unlike planned cities, the *daldongnae* – shaped organically by the urban poor – still retained a spatial logic rooted in the terrain and social life. What Cho saw was not poverty, but beauty born of adaptation.

In these places, he found a kind of modern vernacular – a living, evolving attitude towards space-making that responded instinctively to the land. While conducting his research, Cho got to know the owners of three houses in Sindang-dong and proposed designs to them. In doing so, he treated the urban terrain as a collaborator rather than an obstacle.

Cho carefully considered how his buildings would meet the informal paths. He studied the stairs and intermediate thresholds between inside and out, forming relationships between architecture and alley, between private retreat and shared life. Limited budgets required him to work with local carpenters and even residents themselves. Despite the many constraints, what Cho pursued was not aesthetic perfection, but the possibility of creating spaces that embraced humane living.

These lessons carried over into early projects, including an L-Shaped House (Ilsan, Gyeonggi Province, 1995) and an I-Shaped House (Pyeongchang-dong, Seoul, 1997), where he began to translate vernacular spatial forms into architectural language. Through layout and proportion, he foregrounded the relationship between alley and courtyard, path and neighbour.

The I-Shaped House, based on a layout found in traditional folk dwellings, arranged rooms and *maru* (a wooden floor, often a raised platform, that functions as a communal space) in a single row – allowing air to flow freely through the front and back. The simplicity of the plan also made it easy to position in relation to its surroundings. 'When you have this kind of relationship,' Cho explains, 'a situation is created in which life can unfold. I came to believe that the simpler the architecture, the more beautifully it can accept the reality of everyday life – its flows, its organic moments.'

In both this L-Shaped House and the I-Shaped House, Cho experimented with plan and placement as a way to draw architecture into relationships with the courtyard, the alley and the topography. His aim was never to impose form, but to form relationships.

DESIGN-BUILD AND THE POETICS OF MAKING

After a short period teaching in Germany, Cho returned to Korea in 1994 to begin his first major independent project: a combined home and studio for himself in Seongbuk-dong, a quiet, hilly neighbourhood in northern Seoul. The site was occupied by a run-down Japanese colonial-era house on the verge of collapse. Rather than demolishing it, Cho chose to renovate and transform it, even making it a personal goal to achieve zero construction waste – marking both the beginning of his architectural practice and the start of a lifelong engagement with reuse.

'It was a house that was nearly falling down,' he recalls. 'But there is something incredibly calming about the way old buildings feel. Their naturalness, their informality – I was drawn to that. Because I had to improvise so much, I was able to let my hands and instincts lead. I wanted the building to feel like it still carried traces of touch.'

An old coal shed, roughly constructed at the back of the house, was converted into his studio. Bricks salvaged from a demolished wall were reused as paving stones in a patio area. Rather than masking materials, Cho allowed them to show their age and story. The existing brick and concrete walls were overlaid with new materials: glass and steel plates that revealed, rather than concealed, the layers of time.

Due to budget limitations, Cho carried out much of the construction himself. What began as a necessity soon became a turning point. It was the beginning of his deep understanding of materials, structure and the physical act of building. 'I didn't see economy as something I had to "overcome" in order to achieve a design,' he says. 'Instead, I made it part of the concept. I used materials that were easy to find. I chose methods that were easy to build.'

This attitude defined his early work. He often used stained plywood to achieve a wood effect, Galvalume roofing, and thin steel scaffolding poles as structural columns. These were not glamorous materials – they were inexpensive, commonly used in barns or sheds. But Cho didn't see them as restrictive. Instead, he explored how they could be used precisely and beautifully.

To minimize material waste, he often used building materials at their standard sizes, directly incorporating those dimensions into his design. Even these budget-conscious decisions led to unexpectedly elegant proportions and material juxtapositions. 'More often than not,' he says, 'the most economical way to build turns out to be the most environmentally friendly.'

With this experience of working to low budgets and tough building criteria, Cho began to see the Korean construction industry as a system to be worked with – a field within which he could develop his own aesthetics of practicality. These early lessons became the foundation for a unique way of working – one in which design and construction were no longer separate, but simultaneous: they formed a loop. Cho called this approach 'Re-finding' – a reversal of the conventional process in which you design first, then you build.

As architectural critic Clifford A. Pearson later wrote, 'Cho's architecture has strong foundations in social responsibility.' By working directly with inexpensive and accessible materials, Cho wasn't just saving money – he was articulating a distinctly contemporary Korean aesthetic.

In resisting smooth finishes and perfection, Cho's architecture became more honest. In its exposed structure, it revealed its intent. In its incompleteness, it felt more natural. This restraint and directness echoed the principles of Daoism and traditional Korean aesthetics, in which beauty lies not in decoration, but in the clarity of form and the traces of labour.

What Cho began to build was not only architecture, but also a process. And that process became his philosophy.

VARIATIONS ON SIMPLE BOXES AND THE SPACE IN BETWEEN

Shaped like the Korean letter ㅁ, Concrete Box House (2004) was a watershed moment in Cho's career – the architectural realization of the concepts he had long explored under the theme of experience and perception. Located in Sugok-ri, about an hour's drive from Seoul, and designed as his second home, this house brought to life the square box form he had developed in his graduation thesis. The reason for pursuing such a simple geometric form was clear: to create a space that would contain and heighten experiences of nature.

To achieve this, Cho kept the exterior of the house almost entirely closed off and focused the design inwards. Within the square plan, he created a central courtyard, with similar proportions to those in traditional *hanok* houses. Ten wooden columns reclaimed from redeveloped *hanoks* stood around the perimeter of this courtyard – not merely decorative references, but elements that carried both structural function and emotional memory. While the house clearly evoked the *hanok* experience, its abstract concrete form resisted nostalgia. Rather than replicating a traditional image, it aimed to deliver a sensory relationship with light, air and the open sky.

This project also included a series of bold structural experiments aimed at preserving the purity of the form. Cho wanted to avoid installing waterproofing materials, which would have required a parapet that would break the visual simplicity of the box. Instead, he employed a natural waterproofing technique by manually rubbing the surface of the curing concrete with a trowel. He also dared to connect timber columns directly to concrete walls – despite the risks posed by the different rates of material shrinkage. His deep understanding of how wood contracts and how concrete deforms allowed him to carry out this experiment with confidence.

The results proved successful. The ten wooden columns evenly distributed the structural load without the need for beams. This allowed for a perfectly flat roof without a parapet, and for a volume in which the courtyard became the most dominant sensory space. As the concrete box grew simpler, the natural experiences it invited – shifting light and shadows, falling rain, passing breezes – became more intense.

Designed for a well-known Korean DJ, In-yong Hwang, the Camerata Music Studio (2003) expanded Cho's exploration of box-based forms. With Concrete Box House he created a pure concrete box, but with the Camerata project he began to experiment with combining two or more such boxes. The building comprised two volumes placed side by side, loosely connected with a translucent screen – one serving as a studio and café area, the other as Hwang's private living quarters. The resulting in-between space became not just a circulation zone, but a courtyard for air, water and light to enter – a place for pause and reflection.

Camerata is located in the Heyri Art Valley, an area of Paju known for its thriving creative community. In designing it, Cho aimed to heighten the auditory experience by returning to an architectural memory: the barns of rural Montana. He proposed a darkened interior pierced by a single shaft of light and filled with music. The idea immediately resonated with Hwang, who recalled the sound and light of a salt storage barn from his childhood.

To bring this spatial idea to life, Cho avoided interior columns by suspending the ceiling with wires from above, thus keeping the purity of the box shape intact. The acoustic challenges were resolved creatively: instead of installing sound-absorbing panels, he left the concrete ceiling roughened with trowel marks during the curing process, allowing it to serve a dual function as both surface and sound absorber.

Between the two box volumes, Cho created a courtyard that functioned as a garden, a buffer and a place of sensory experience. After Concrete Box House and Camerata, Cho continued to develop what became known as his 'Box Series'. Houses composed of two or three boxes followed, each time exploring how the spaces between volumes could form new kinds of experience and relationships.

As the series progressed, the forms began to bend and twist. The once-static box started to respond to topography. Linear geometries gave way to soft curves. These spatial evolutions were not stylistic shifts, but architectural responses to terrain. What started as abstraction gradually became organic movement.

Cho's exploration of simple forms also expanded into structural and material research. His early concrete experiments were followed by investigations into wire structures. Projects such as the Kiswire Memorial and Training Centre (2014) in Busan – which was created for the Kiswire company as an exhibition space primarily dedicated to its speciality, steel wire products – later demonstrated how wire could be employed not only as structural reinforcement, but as a spatial material in its own right.

The integration of construction method, structural logic and craftsmanship became another essential identity in Cho's work. It was no longer just about form – it was about how buildings were made, and how their making could be felt in every detail.

DESIGNING THE GROUND

Byoung Cho's exploration into architectural archetypes ultimately led to the creation of Earth House (2009), also located in Sugok-ri. In this project, the box form was boldly driven deep into the earth, until the architectural volume disappeared altogether. Much like Korea's traditional rural houses, in which walls were formed by compacting soil, Earth House was constructed almost entirely from rammed earth, creating a deeply sunken courtyard. In both scale and spatial composition, it carried the emotional resonance of the *hanok*. While the project began from Cho's innate familiarity with earth, it was driven by his belief that simplifying space allows one to sense the sky, the stars, the trees and the wind more vividly. As the form receded into the ground, the surrounding stimuli were pared away, and what remained was an experience filtered through an open sky. In Earth House, Cho was not designing a building – he was designing the ground itself.

This approach continued in Jipyoung Guesthouse (2018), in Geoje, South Gyeongsang Province, which was embedded into a sloped site facing the ocean. In order not to disturb the sea view from the point of entry, Cho cut part of the guesthouse into the cliff. This was not merely a gesture of restraint, but an act of designing the site as a whole. He took advantage of the topography and made the guesthouse a literal extension of it. Long horizontal lines stretching towards the sea divided the volume into six accommodation units, dissolving the solid box form entirely and extending it as part of the land itself.

What's fascinating is that, for Cho, the ground is not an abstract concept. It is a tangible, material entity – an active subject of design. For him, architecture begins with reading the land, interpreting it and designing in unison with it. This approach has remained consistent since his earliest works. Unlike traditional Korean architecture, which harmonized with terrain through passive adaptation, today's urban landscape in Korea has often been ruptured or damaged by rapid industrialization and development. Cho sees the ground not as a given, but as something that must be repaired, re-articulated and redesigned.

Just as pine trees have traditionally been planted along Korea's coastlines to block harsh sea winds, Cho seeks to understand what must be preserved and what must be complemented, how a site's original flows can be restored. In the U-Shaped House (Yangpyeong, Gyeonggi Province, 2002), which fronted a busy street, he built an earthen berm to shield the entrance and brought the gentle slope of the land into the building's interior, dissolving boundaries between site and structure. These efforts are an early example of Cho actively designing the ground rather than merely adapting to it.

This interest in topography later expanded into the urban scale, as seen in the 4th Seoul Biennale of Architecture and Urbanism, for which Cho served as General Director in 2023. His core question was: how might we recover the forgotten mountain trails, water routes and wind corridors of old Hanyang? ('Hanyang' is the historical name for Seoul.) His proposal centred on reconnecting Seoul's natural systems – its terrain, rivers and air currents – to create a more walkable, breathable and physically comfortable city. This wasn't just about responding to site, but about asking how we might restore the ground itself in a high-density metropolis – and how architecture must evolve to meet that task.

Cho's book, *Byoung Cho: My Life as an Architect in Seoul* (2023), reflects these ideas as well. In it, he shares his thoughts on the natural landscapes of Seoul – the mountains, rivers and sites of his childhood – and the buildings he has created in dialogue with them.

'I believe in the importance of the natural environment, the cultural environment, and their context,' he once said. 'Above all, I care deeply about the physical context – topography, wind and water.' The ground, as he defines it, is not an abstract or poetic metaphor. It is a material reality – one that directly shapes our spatial experience. And so, when Cho builds up land or reconnects a severed flow, he demonstrates that, for him, architecture and the ground are not separate entities, but a continuous whole.

Starting with the Tilt Roof House (Yangpyeong, Gyeonggi Province, 2014), Cho's concrete boxes began to find greater freedom. In this project, the slope of the site was resolved by bending the roof, creating a new rooftop surface that served as a kind of courtyard. In Sloped Roof House (2024), on Jeju Island, the roof itself became a new topography – rising from the ground as if it were part of it, to create a space of shelter and intimacy beneath the land. In Cho's work, where interpreting and responding to the land is always the first act of design, concrete roofs and platforms began to play an active role in shaping the ground. This was a physical, three-dimensional interpretation of the earth, with concrete becoming part of the land – its extension and its form.

EMBRACING IMPERFECTION: THE AESTHETICS OF ROUGH SPONTANEITY

'I believe that there is a genre of aesthetics that we have long neglected,' says Cho. 'An aesthetic born of yielding to nature – where comfort, humour and an improvisational spirit come together to form solutions, not by control, but by release. I think it's time we paid attention to that.'

In his way of handling such comfort and humour, Cho accepts the unknown. Rather than striving for perfectly tuned order, he seeks out an architecture that captures the beauty of the unpredictable. In Korea, where traditional methods of construction and the craft-based architectural industry have largely been severed from the present, this willingness to engage with uncertainty becomes, for Cho, a way to formulate a new, modern regionalism.

He finds a poignant reference in the *maksabal*, a simple bowl that was commonly used during the Joseon dynasty. Rapidly and intuitively shaped by the hands of a skilled potter, the bowl was valued not only for its practicality, but also for the unintentional elegance found in its utilitarian form. In its spontaneous making and unassuming presence, Cho sees a reflection of the Korean spirit. The *maksabal* bowl and the moon jar, like the Goryeo celadon, embody a beauty that emerges not from symmetry or control, but from skill that has transcended technique. In these objects, Cho searches for the root of Korean aesthetics and continues to ask how such a quality might be made architectural.

This is why he persistently searches for terms to describe these qualities – phrases like 'the aesthetics of *mahk*' – in order to explain the distinctive character of Korean architecture. His aim is to articulate the spatial essence that arises from physical elements such as wind, water, light and soil – qualities that give Korean architecture its deep sense of naturalness and comfort.

As Professor Hyungmin Pai of the University of Seoul – a critic and curator – writes, 'Rough spontaneity demands the highest level of skill and discipline.' Behind Cho's seemingly simple forms lie deliberate, rigorous and often experimental processes. His architecture does not emerge from ease, but from craftsmanship sharpened by decades of inquiry. And this is why critics often use paradoxical expressions to describe his work: the convergence of organicism and abstraction, or, as Mark Rakatansky describes it, 'refinement in the roughness, casualness within refinement'.

Cho embraces the two extremes of Korean naturalism and modernist abstraction. And indeed, at the heart of Cho's architecture lies a sustained, patient exploration of Korean culture, Eastern philosophy and architectural origin. Rather than building around theory, he builds around experience – sunlight, shadows, breezes and the quiet emptiness in between.

Perhaps it is not grand architectural discourse, but the courtyard of his house, the covered walkway in his office, or the filtered light in the interstitial space between buildings that gives us the clearest glimpse into Cho's vision. Through these voids, we might sense something Korea has lost in its accelerated urban development: the original form of space.

In the design of his houses, Cho often works with spatial scales remembered by the body: a single *pyeong* (about 3.3 m^2 or 36 sq. ft) – just large enough for a person to lie down comfortably – and the square of sky seen above a courtyard recall the scale of a *hanok* yard. His houses, gently settled into the land, attuned to the slope of the ground and framed by the terrain, offer warmth, quiet and the possibility of stillness. In doing so, they present a practical and poetic alternative to the spatial amnesia of contemporary Korean cities.

Cho goes beyond simply making architecture disappear into the ground. He seeks to repair, reform and rebuild land that has been damaged or erased. For him, the ground is not a neutral setting – it is a material and physical reality to be shaped. His architecture unfolds as an extension of the ground itself. And to achieve the quiet restraint of his concrete forms, he embraces new uses of modern materials, takes bold structural steps and brings his deep understanding of craft to bear on every detail.

Through the disciplined modesty of concrete and his organically attuned response to terrain, Cho creates spaces that are not only economical in gesture, but deeply emotional in experience. They speak softly, yet they resonate powerfully. They hold light and silence. They don't speak in metaphors, but in sensations of space.

MAK AND BIUM
IMPERFECTION AND EMPTINESS IN KOREAN AESTHETICS

BYOUNG CHO

The Korean worldview is underlined by a characteristic spontaneity. Elements that to the uninitiated may pass by overlooked, often reveal a rich emotive resonance on deeper inspection. This subtle tone infuses Korean space, asserted often through a directness that permeates design. The resulting aesthetic capacity of these conditions is conveyed particularly well in one specific word, *mak*.

Commonly used to imply a vulgarity or crudeness, *mak* elicits something overlooked, castigated in a hasty indifference to finesse – *makgeolli*, for instance, is an unrefined state of *soju*, a smooth mainstay Korean drink. Yet this notion is more than just a word; *mak* is a mode of thought, a temperament, which hides everywhere in plain sight. So many things, from our food, to our traditional dance and even to our understanding of the city, manifest a certain matter-of-factness about how we approach being. Korean aesthetics endorse a distinct fondness towards the unexpected. Such is the special condition of Korean culture: a solemn abjection of the refinement for which so many others strive. We value humility that bears witness not only to a work itself, but also to an embracing compassion for the context in which we realize it – be it an object or a building.

Korean architecture derives an overall character from a strikingly unrehearsed act. This includes every part of the building's identity, from the material to the tectonic. At Byeongsanseowon, a 16th-century Confucian school, you will find withered columns lifting the weight of the building's mass above a ravine. Raw and seemingly unfinished, these are not a concession to ageing, but an aesthetic statement. Their splintering perimeters speak, almost literally, to something more than the disintegration brought on by time, and instead suggest an innate tactility, an emptiness that is wholeheartedly Korean. The wavering irregularities of the Byeongsanseowon columns expound a kind of emotional depth implicit in the architecture. Their deformed whimsicalities resist being painted over or sanded down and are welcomed for their ability to endow a space with exciting rawness – their asymmetry is as if they were laid by the intuitively unthinking hands of a potter.

Like sombre statues from long ago, a tangibility invites those who encounter them to sense intimately the soul of the building. It seeps between the uneven stone plinth below each column, individuated by their oblong arrangement. Sinking into the sea of rough sand that covers the floor, the tender fragility of the columns' misalignment fills the space with an energy of dislocation. Where in Western architecture an axis of symmetry might spatialize a reassurance of hierarchy, Korean structures feel off-kilter. The visitor is let free in this vague but declarative aura, at one with the space as it is itself with nature. This milieu is constantly alive with a vivacity of movement and slippage. When I stand between the columns, I feel not only the softly misshapen figure of their silhouettes or the depth of their wooden materiality, but something more significant. There resonates an ephemeral vacancy brewing in their imperfection.

We call this state *bium*, literally 'emptiness'. *Mak* produces this sense of emptiness, a deference to surroundings that grants testimony to both context and material. This emptiness is more than the simple vacancy of space. When potters do their craftwork, for example, they might whisk a clay piece haphazardly in seconds. The swift liveliness of their act obliges a candour between author and work. Haste overcomes perfection, enticing a state of unadulterated creation between author and medium where no preconceptions may exist.

Lee Ufan, an influential Korean painter and theorist, identifies moon jars – renowned Joseon dynasty (1392–1897) pottery – as asserting an honesty devoid of pretension. Sculpted from two hemispherical bowls joined at the middle, their lopsided profiles approach near abstraction. Through this rawness, these objects 'lack completeness and presence as an art work' and yet they attain 'an impressive affinity to [their] surroundings'.

In traditional Korean *hanok* houses, a courtyard – a space of literal emptiness in the architectural sense – anchors the household with a public void. Their architecture is in different ways saturated by both the calm vacancy of *bium* and by the informal directness of *mak*. Their walls are textured by spontaneous constraints and site conditions, not overarching ideals and concepts. In lieu of precise arrangement, openings fit between the warped wooden contours of beams, and rafters remain unprocessed where Japanese or Western buildings might prefer the abstraction of sawn wooden units. This impression persists in the contrast between the rough concrete for which Seoul has become famous, and the white Minimalist spaces of contemporary Japanese architecture. The *hanok* home finds a unique personality in its uncompromising faith in respect of a negotiation between spontaneity and space, a serene balance between the acts of making and being.

In these homes, architectural elements are shuffled within the unrehearsed nature of their surroundings, tilting and shearing between their organic boundaries, just as the building itself snuggles into the hillside. Truly Korean architecture often acquiesces to its natural surroundings, relinquishing the hilltop, stretching subtly across the rolling valleys below. The culture has come to reflect this informality towards our heavily mountainous landscape through architectural 'co-operation'. These topographical challenges have strongly determined the character of Korean design. About this, Lee makes another intriguing distinction: that it is not Korea's quantity of mountains (plenty of countries encompass such mountain ranges), but the quality of their arrangement that influences the Korean experience: 'Korea's natural environment isn't very expansive or especially beautiful ... [rather it] is a living environment that is temperate, easy to adjust to ... much like a mother's embrace'.

To exemplify this, we might visit the Buseoksa Temple, perhaps one of the most famous traditional religious sites in Korea, where one can feel how the arrangement of the compound fuses into the mountains. Though prominent examples of Chinese and Japanese Buddhist temples from the same period follow clear axial arrangements regardless of terrain, the architecture at Buseoksa melds with nature in the form of elegant pragmatism. Buildings skew from entrance to shrine, leaving distinct voids between their edges. Rather than struggling against topographic challenges, the temple acquiesces in the entropy of nature, underscoring an inclination across Korean architecture to explore the possibilities of a site before imposing extraneous ideas.

In their make-do posture, these artefacts of architecture define a naturalistic comprehension of the world, akin to the Confucian Seonbi doctrines that contextualized them during the Joseon dynasty, frugal but imbued with affection, connecting craft and emotion. From the flick of a *maksabal* potter, to the casualness of a temple's site plan, to the rawness of a *hanok* beam, Korean culture revels in the process of creation, where an intuitive nature of making finds aesthetic prominence in a literal expression, a humble bluntness between crafting and object.

Mak is sensual and intuitive, celebrating the act of creation instead of adhering strictly to dogmatic principles. Impressed into its material form is the pure craftwork of a human creator without the hubris of perfection, unlike the preplanned designs of China and Japan. Where those styles articulate consistency through established principles, *mak* has historically allowed for a vast diversity in Korean design. This lineage is united not by an aesthetic uniformity but through kind-hearted imperfection.

Because it engages the transient nature of being, Western spectators might note that *mak* is not unlike the Japanese concept of *wabi-sabi*. However, there are some important differences that distinguish Korean design from that of its neighbours. Although both value the inaccurate splendour of the human touch, Japanese examples are generally crafted in the image of gentle imperfection. A Korean proverb goes so far as to ironically place Japan's 1592 invasion of Korea as a consequence of *daimyō* Toyotomi Hideyoshi's obsession for *maksabal*. A playful exaggeration, it is nonetheless the case that the Japanese returned, accompanying a large group of expert Korean artisans whose work would hold immense ramifications for the country's aesthetic development. This begins to contextualize the Japanese preoccupation with a rough appearance in and of itself, rather than with the process whence it emerges.

In Korean designs this humanness is not a prearranged aesthetic ideal, but an excitedly spontaneous derivative of their creation. In Korean *seungmu* dance, for example, performers break from the rhythm of their performances to adopt spur-of-the-moment alterations in choreography. This nonchalance distinguishes us from the careful eloquence of Western aesthetics, as well as from the prearranged compositions of Japan and China. Where the trajectory of historical crafts in other cultures pursued a studied refinement, Korean crafts hold little regard for straightforward perfection. If we study the docility of the Zen gardens at the Ryōan-ji temple or the muted refinement of *chashitsu* (tea houses) in Japan, we encounter environments whose unassuming temperament is in appearance only. Their humble demeanours are, in truth, the product of considerable planning beforehand.

While this coarse spontaneity has become less outwardly apparent in Korea since the first decade of the 20th century, soon after the end of the Joseon dynasty, it continues to pervade Korean identity in our modestly unadorned cuisine, in the briskness of the city and in the primordial crests of the mountains that still define our landscape. Contemporary Korean art can be traced back to these traditional ideas. Artists such as Seobo Park and Lee Ufan paint with an attention to the informality between fabrication and emotion that relentlessly harbours this rawness. Even in Modernist architecture in Korea, we witness what Hyungmin Pai has described as 'Korean identity in spaces focusing on qualities of emptiness, non-existence and *madang* [traditional courtyards]'. As a new generation has taken the reins of architecture in Korea, many – myself included – have considered anew what it means to design from this standpoint. In my own work, a vocabulary of rough materials and a process focused on the intimacy of construction and detailing attempt to engage the spontaneity and honest beauty for which *mak* allows.

Mak remains, though outwardly less apparent, as an emotive backdrop to Korean identity. If its traditional conception presided over an ambiguity between process and creation, perhaps the contemporary version of this attitude lies in an ability to make us consider the depth of life, to surprise us with its vivacity in a way that might provoke afresh the kind of close thought and emotional consideration so deeply embedded in our history.

This article by Byoung Cho was originally published by *The Architectural Review*, February 2018

NOTES

PAGES

306 'Earth Architect' by Jin-young Lim

All quotations from Byoung Cho are taken from interviews with the author, except those detailed below.

306 'These ideas extend outwards into notions such as contemporary vernacular, Cho's "design-build" method...': 'Design-build' is derived from a remark made by Byoung Cho in an interview with Clifford A. Pearson, specifically referring to the 'design-build process': 'I call this "re-finding",' says Cho, 'reversing the design-build process. So, it's build, then design.' See Clifford A. Pearson, 'Byoungsoo Cho Challenges Norms in the Way Design and Construction Work Together', Design Vanguard, *Architectural Record*, December 2004, p. 140

309 'While researching the urban fabric of Sindang-dong, Cho sought to learn the principles of traditional Korean architecture from Professor Shi-chun Jung': see Professor Shi-chun Jung, 'Spatial Analysis of Korean Traditional Village and Modern Natural Settlement', in Byoung-Soo Cho Architects, *Making of Architecture I*, Seoul, March 1997

310 'Cho's architecture has strong foundations in social responsibility': see Clifford A. Pearson, 'Byoungsoo Cho Challenges Norms in the Way Design and Construction Work Together', Design Vanguard, *Architectural Record*, December 2004, p. 140

313 'As Professor Hyungmin Pai of the University of Seoul – a critic and curator – writes, "Rough spontaneity demands the highest level of skill and discipline"': see Byoung-Soo Cho, *BCHO Partners – Cho Byoung-Soo*, 공간서가 (*SPACE*), Seoul, 2024

313 'And this is why critics often use paradoxical expressions to describe his work: the convergence of organicism and abstraction, or, as Mark Rakatansky describes it, "refinement in the roughness, casualness within refinement"': Mark Rakatansky, *Refinement in the Roughness, Casualness within Refinement*, *SPACE*, Seoul, April 2007

PICTURE CREDITS

All ink drawings by Byoung Cho

PAGES

2	Wooseop Hwang
11	Sergio Pirrone
15	Sua Kim
18–29	Wooseop Hwang
33	Jaegyeong Kim
36/49	Wooseop Hwang
55	Sua Kim
58–69	Jong Oh Kim
73	Sua Kim
76–87	Wooseop Hwang
91	Jinwon Park
94–101	Wooseop Hwang
105	Jaegyeong Kim
108	(from the top) Wooseop Hwang, Kim Yongkwan, Wooseop Hwang, Wooseop Hwang, Wooseop Hwang, Kim Yongkwan
109	(from the top) Kim Yongkwan, Wooseop Hwang, Wooseop Hwang, Wooseop Hwang, Wooseop Hwang, Wooseop Hwang
110/121	Wooseop Hwang
128–35	Wooseop Hwang
142–55	Wooseop Hwang
159	Sua Kim
162–71	Wooseop Hwang
175	Sua Kim
178	(from the top) Sua Kim, Sergio Pirrone (all)
179–89	Sergio Pirrone
193	Sua Kim
196–207	Wooseop Hwang
211	Sergio Pirrone
214	(from the top) Sergio Pirrone, Sergio Pirrone, Sergio Pirrone, Youngtae Park, Sergio Pirrone, Sergio Pirrone
215	(from the top) Youngtae Park, Sergio Pirrone, Youngtae Park, Jeong Park, Sergio Pirrone, Youngtae Park
216–23	Sergio Pirrone
229	Sergio Pirrone
232–43	Sergio Pirrone
247	Sergio Pirrone
250	(from the top) Sergio Pirrone, Sergio Pirrone, Sergio Pirrone, Sergio Pirrone, Team Virals, Team Virals
251	(from the top) Sergio Pirrone, Team Virals, Team Virals, Team Virals, Team Virals, Sergio Pirrone
252–53	Sergio Pirrone
254–55	Team Virals
256–61	Sergio Pirrone
268–79	Wooseop Hwang
314–15	Youngtae Park

ACKNOWLEDGMENTS

I would like to express my gratitude to Lucas Dietrich, Augusta Pownall, Aman Phull, Rebecca Pearson and the team at Thames & Hudson.

The works in these pages were only possible with the help of the people at BCHO Partners, especially my three partners, Jihyun Lee, Kyoungjin Hoong and Jayoon Yoon. Special thanks also go to Michele Maria Riva, Chaelim Park and Sua Kim for putting together the text and materials necessary to realize the book, and for their passionate enthusiasm.

BIOGRAPHIES

BYOUNG CHO

Since founding BCHO Partners in Seoul in 1994, Byoung Cho has built a reputation as the key architect driving the expansion of one of the world's most densely populated cities. Influenced by Korea's rich aesthetic tradition, Cho utilizes understated forms to design buildings that yield powerful and subtle experiences for their inhabitants, with a strong regard for nature and sustainability.

Over the past thirty years, BCHO Partners has established itself as a leading architectural firm in South Korea, with projects such as the Hyundai Cheonan Global Learning Center, South Cape and Jipyoung Guesthouse. Cho's work has garnered numerous accolades, including the AIA Honor Award (2003, 2013) and the Kim Swoo Geun Architectural Award (2010), as well as international awards such as the Red Dot Award and iF Design Award (2021). Cho has also been a prominent academic voice, teaching at institutions such as Montana State University and Harvard, and serving as curator for the Gwangju Biennale in 2009, and Seoul Biennale of Architecture and Urbanism (SBAU) in 2023.

In recent years, Cho has returned to his roots in art, dedicating time to his studio practice. Inspired by the *maksabal*, a traditional Korean ceramic with a rough, unfinished appearance, Cho developed the concept of *mahk*, a spontaneous, humble approach to creation that he applies to both his paintings and his architecture. In his art, he explores organic shapes through brushstrokes on rice paper, capturing movement and energy, much as he seeks to capture moments of experience in his architectural work. His painting process is, as he describes it, 'guided by spontaneous action', in the same way he approaches each architectural project with openness and a willingness to embrace imperfection.

JIN-YOUNG LIM

Jin-young Lim is an architectural journalist who has curated, edited and led a wide range of projects in architecture. Having worked as a journalist for *C3KOREA* and *SPACE*, she has gone on to contribute articles for publications such as *MARK MAGAZINE*, *AR Asia Pacific* and *DB Magazine*. Since 2012, she has been director of Open House Seoul, part of a worldwide network of sixty organizations hosting festivals and conversations about architecture. In 2021 she co-curated the exhibition 'Homely Talk: Byoung-Soo Cho X Wook Choi', and in 2023 she was co-curator for the Guest Cities Exhibition at the Seoul Biennale of Architecture and Urbanism.

On the cover: (front) Jipyoung Guesthouse, Changho-ri, Sadeung-myeon, Geoje-si, Gyeongsangnam-do, South Korea. Photograph by Sergio Pirrone; (back) Ginkgo Tree House, Tongui-dong, Jongno-gu, Seoul, South Korea. Photograph by Wooseop Hwang

Frontispiece: Concrete Box House, Sugok-ri, jipyeong-myeon, Yangpyeong-gun, Gyeonggi-do, South Korea

pp. 314–15: Jipyoung Guesthouse, Changho-ri, Sadeung-myeon, Geoje-si, Gyeongsangnam-do, South Korea

First published in the United Kingdom in 2026 by
Thames & Hudson Ltd, 6–24 Britannia Street,
London WC1X 9JD

First published in the United States of America in 2026 by
Thames & Hudson Inc., 500 Fifth Avenue, New York,
New York 10110

Picture credits can be found on p. 321.

EU Authorized Representative: Interart S.A.R.L.
19 rue Charles Auray, 93500 Pantin, Paris, France
productsafety@thameshudson.co.uk
interart.fr

A CIP catalogue record for this book is available from the British Library

Library of Congress Control Number 2025944570

ISBN 978-0-500-02936-7
01

Printed and bound in China by C&C Offset Printing Co. Ltd